IN THE STUDIO

with ANGELA WALTERS

Machine-Quilting Design Concepts
Add Movement, Contrast, Depth & More

stashBOOKS®
an imprint of C&T Publishing

Text copyright © 2012 by Angela Walters

Photography and Artwork copyright © 2012 by C&T Publishing, Inc.

Publisher: Amy Marson

Creative Director: Gailen Runge

Art Director: Kristy Zacharias

Editors: Liz Aneloski and Phyllis Elving

Technical Editors: Sadhana Wray and Mary E. Flynn

Cover/Book Designer: April Mostek

Production Coordinator: Jessica Jenkins

Production Editor: S. Michele Fry

Illustrator: Wendy Mathson

Photography by Christina Carty-Francis and Diane Pedersen of C&T Publishing, Inc., unless otherwise noted

Published by Stash Books, an imprint of C&T Publishing, Inc., P.O. Box 1456, Lafayette, CA 94549

Library of Congress Cataloging-in-Publication Data

Walters, Angela, 1979-

In the studio with Angela Walters : machine quilting design concepts - add movement, contrast, depth & more.

pages cm

ISBN 978-1-60705-655-3 (soft cover)

1. Quilting--Design. 2. Machine quilting. I. Title.

TT835.W35655 2012

746.46--dc23

2012013353

Printed in China

10 9 8 7 6 5 4 3 2

Dedication
To Jeremy, Drake, Cloe, and Hailey ... my biggest supporters!

Acknowledgments
This book wouldn't be possible without the people who helped make most of the quilts:

Georgieanna Martin

Jessica Harrison

Mary Workman

Shea Henderson

Alex Ledgerwood

Kathy Limpic

Emily Cier

A very special thanks goes out to my **editors and friends at C&T Publishing:** Susanne, Liz, Sadhana, April, and a dozen others behind the scenes who have worked so hard to make me feel like a member of their family.

A final thanks goes out to **Robert Kaufman Fabrics** for supplying the fabric for the quilts in this book.

Contents

Preface

As a designer, I love what I do and am very grateful
to work in the independent craft world where I have
a chance to cross paths with other inspired designers
and creators. I had the great opportunity of meeting
Angela last year during one of our Quilt Markets, and I
was immediately taken by her enthusiasm, passion, and
warmth. We excitedly discussed the show and our new
projects and bonded as we learned more about each
other. This quickly led to a "show and tell" where I gave
her the tour of my booth, and then we ran over to Tula
Pink's booth so I could see Angela's unique quilting
technique and style. WOW! I was immediately smitten
with her skills and fresh approach. Since that day, we've
been great supporters of one another's work.

That is why I am so honored and proud to tell you
about this book. Angela is an artist, and her unique
perspective on modern quilting will unlock a world of
new ideas and experiences for you. First and foremost,
she believes that machine quilting is another layer of
art on a quilt, not just a function of utility. I love this!
She presents loads of beautiful eye candy, and plenty
of inspiration to open the door for your creativity.
Angela's goal is to empower you and get you to think
differently, to encourage you to experiment, and ulti-
mately to enhance your projects. You'll love every tidbit
of beauty, design, and technique, and you'll especially
love meeting her. Enjoy, and happy, happy quilting!

~Amy Butler, *textile designer & author of* Style Stitches

Introduction

The Form and Function of Quilting

What does this mean, anyway—the form and function of quilting? Quilting is both a functional element and an art form. The basic function of quilting is to hold together the three layers of a quilt. But just because quilting is functional doesn't mean that it can't also be an art. In fact, I often refer to the quilting as another layer of art on a quilt.

So what does *this* mean? How can quilting add to the quilt? That's exactly what this book is for! I am going to show you how to use quilting to achieve different effects in quilt tops. Quilting can add depth, for instance. Quilting can tell a story, and quilting can add movement to a quilt top.

Each chapter of this book demonstrates a different use of quilting. I've included tips and ideas to help you achieve the results you want. Each chapter also includes directions for a quilt designed especially to use the techniques that you've just learned in that chapter. These quilts range in size from small to large, and they use a number of different techniques. Of course, you don't have to make the quilts in this book—you can practice the quilting designs on plain pieces of fabric or apply the suggestions to quilts you make in the future. You also don't have to quilt the projects exactly as I've shown. Feel free to try out your own ideas on the quilt tops.

A Few Clarifications

First of all, I'm not against allover quilting designs. There are some quilts for which that is the best choice. For instance, quilts with a lot of little pieces that tend to blend together are great candidates for an allover design.

Second, you don't need a longarm quilting machine to use the techniques in this book. I am always quick to point out that I'm a machine quilter, not just a longarm quilter. Although a longarm quilting machine is what I use, don't feel that you must have one before you can quilt custom designs. That said, if you are a prolific quilter or undertake a lot of large projects, it may be worth looking into buying or renting a longarm. It makes the quilting a little easier.

Finally, in this book I suggest concepts that work best for *me*. They may or may not be the best for you. If you come across an idea you don't love, tweak it a bit to make it your own. Quilting is a lot like handwriting. There are a lot of ways to write the letter A, just as there are a lot of ways to quilt a swirl. Make these ideas that you own!

My hope is that this book will make you think of quilting as more than just a way to keep the layers of a quilt together. I want you to feel empowered to experiment with different uses of quilting and different methods. I want you to love quilting as much as I do—it's the part that's the most fun! So here's to happy quilting in your future.

QUILTING
TELLS A STORY

Sometimes when I am stumped about how to quilt a project, I ask the piecer to tell me the story behind the quilt. When I find out why someone made a quilt and the important things about it, deciding how to quilt it is usually a lot easier.

You can use the story behind a quilt as the inspiration for your quilting designs. Or you can use the quilting itself to help tell the story. Either way, this is one of the most gratifying ways to quilt a piece, and it will help make the quilt come to life!

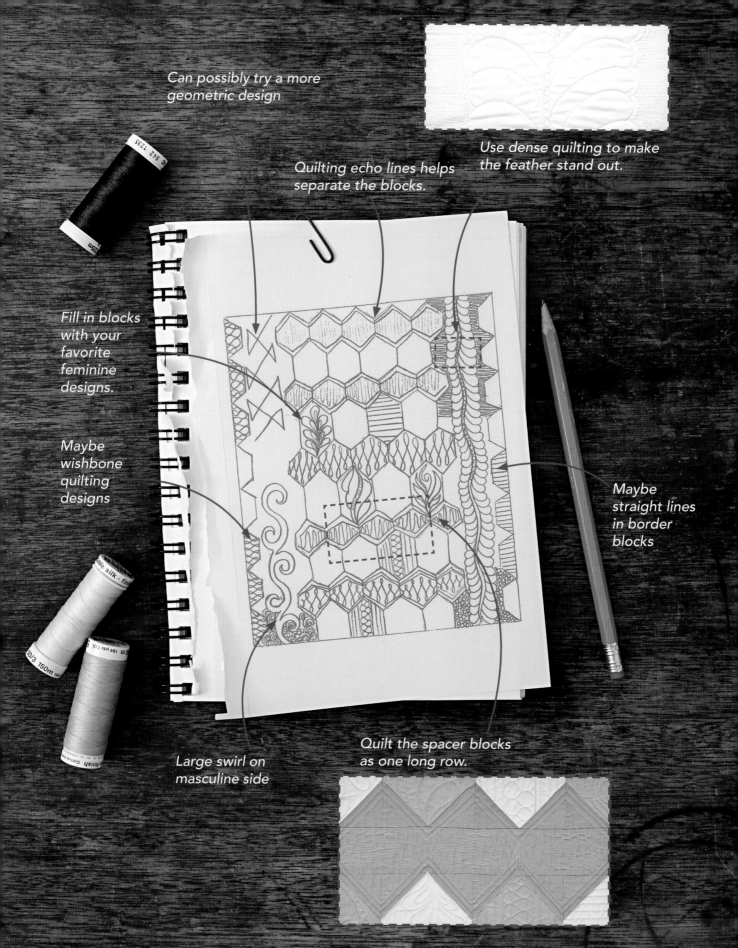

Can possibly try a more geometric design

Quilting echo lines helps separate the blocks.

Use dense quilting to make the feather stand out.

Fill in blocks with your favorite feminine designs.

Maybe wishbone quilting designs

Maybe straight lines in border blocks

Large swirl on masculine side

Quilt the spacer blocks as one long row.

Using Words and Designs to Tell a Story

When you want to tell the story literally, use meaningful words as the quilting design. This isn't a new method, of course. Quilters have been quilting words on quilts since at least the 1800s. It's a great way to convey a message or add meaningful information.

I made the *Ribbons* quilt in honor of two women in my family who battled cancer. One of them won her battle, but sadly her sister succumbed to the disease. I incorporated cancer awareness ribbons for both cancers into the quilt top, but I wanted the quilting to help tell their story, too.

I quilted several words to describe both of the women—*sister, mother, friend, daughter, fighter, supporter*. For an extra-special touch, I carefully quilted the words *sisters forever* backward on the top so that they can be read when the quilt is viewed from the back.

I didn't use words alone to tell the story. I also added angel wings to the green ribbon to show that one of the women is no longer with us.

Even though the quilt top makes a strong statement by itself, the quilting really helps add to the background story and makes this quilt even more special.

Quilting Cursive Letters

Using words as a quilting design is easy and fun! Cursive letters are the easiest to quilt because you can just free-hand them as you go. Some letters are tricky—such as lowercase *i* and *t*—but with practice you can do it. You just quilt the words and then fill in the extra areas with a meander or other loose design.

When quilting cursive words, you can make up the design as you go. If you want the designs to look more even, you can mark them first. Try marking words to go in all directions.

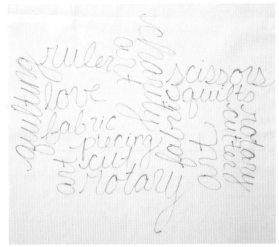

Marking the words before you start will help keep you on track.

Quilting Block Letters

Stitching cursive words to blend in with the rest of the quilting is great, but if you want the words to show up more, block letters are best. They take a little more work, but they aren't really that much harder to quilt. Mark out the letters with chalk or another marking tool, and then quilt around them.

Telling Another Kind of Story

Telling a story with quilting doesn't have to be literal. It can be more of a hint or an inspiration for the design.

For instance, I once quilted a quilt that was made with large orange circles. The piecer told me she had made it in honor of her husband's marriage proposal to her under a full moon. Knowing her story made it easier to select my quilting designs. I quilted various sizes of circles to replicate the phases of the moon.

Someone looking at the quilt wouldn't know the story behind the quilting design, but the piecer did. It made the quilt that much more memorable for her.

He Says, She Says

FINISHED SIZE: 66½˝ × 81½˝

Pieced by Alexandra Ledgerwood and machine quilted by Angela Walters

I often toyed with the idea of making a quilt in which each half is quilted in a different style or design. When I decided to go for it, I knew I needed a pattern that left a lot of open space for many different designs. The result is *He Says, She Says.*

One side of this quilt has feminine designs, the most noticeable of them being the large feather that climbs along the side border. To complete the story, I quilted the left side with more masculine-feeling designs. Along the border, I quilted a unifying swirl design.

MATERIALS

Light tan: 1¼ yards

Dark tan: ⅞ yard

Light green: 1⅛ yards

Dark green: 1⅛ yards

Cream: 2½ yards

Dark brown: 1¼ yards, for border and binding

Backing: 5 yards

Batting: 74″ × 89″

CUTTING

Light tan

Cut 7 strips 3½″ × width of fabric; subcut into 60 squares 3½″ × 3½″; and 6 rectangles 3½″ × 6½″.

Cut 3 rectangles 3½″ × 36½″.

Dark tan

Cut 5 strips 3½″ × width of fabric; subcut into 48 squares 3½″ × 3½″.

Cut 2 rectangles 3½″ × 36½″.

Light green

Cut 5 strips 6½″ × width of fabric; subcut into

    3 rectangles 6½″ × 9½″

    6 rectangles 6½″ × 12½″

    4 rectangles 6½″ × 15½″

Dark green

Cut 5 strips 6½″ × width of fabric; subcut into

    2 rectangles 6½″ × 9½″

    4 rectangles 6½″ × 12½″

    6 rectangles 6½″ × 15½″

Cream

Cut 2 strips 12½″ × 81½″ (cut along the length of the fabric for a continuous piece).

Cut 4 strips 3½″ × 81½″; subcut into

    48 squares 3½″ × 3½″

    2 rectangles 3½″ × 9½″

    4 rectangles 3½″ × 12½″

    4 rectangles 3½″ × 15½″

Dark brown (border and binding)

Cut 2 strips 9½″ × width of fabric; subcut into 18 rectangles 3½″ × 9½″.

Cut 8 strips 2¼″ × width of fabric for binding.

Making and Assembling the Blocks

1. Sew the blocks according to the following chart, using the quick corner-triangle technique used in the *Spools* quilt (Making the Blocks, page 50).

Rectangle	Squares	Block	Finished size
6½″ × 15½″		Make 6.	6½″ × 15½″
6½″ × 12½″		Make 4.	6½″ × 12½″
6½″ × 9½″		Make 2.	6½″ × 9½″
6½″ × 15½″		Make 4.	6½″ × 15½″
6½″ × 12½″		Make 6.	6½″ × 12½″
6½″ × 9½″		Make 3.	6½″ × 9½″

Rectangle	Squares	Block	Finished size
3½″ × 12½″		Make 2.	3½″ × 12½″
3½″ × 12½″		Make 2.	3½″ × 12½″
3½″ × 15½″		Make 2.	3½″ × 15½″
3½″ × 15½″		Make 2.	3½″ × 15½″
3½″ × 9½″		Make 1.	3½″ × 9½″
3½″ × 9½″		Make 1.	3½″ × 9½″
3½″ × 6½″		Make 6.	3½″ × 6½″

2. Follow the diagram below to sew the blocks into rows and then to sew the rows together.

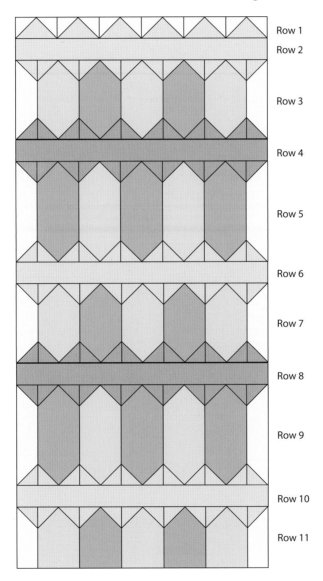

Row 1
Row 2
Row 3
Row 4
Row 5
Row 6
Row 7
Row 8
Row 9
Row 10
Row 11

Making the Borders

1. Sew a 12½″ × 81½″ background strip to each side of the quilt top.

2. Using the 3½″ × 9½″ dark brown rectangles and the 3½″ × 3½″ squares of background fabric, make 18 border blocks.

Make 18.

Finished size
3½″ × 9½″

3. Matching the short edges, sew the border blocks together to make 2 strips of 9 blocks each.

4. Sew a border strip to each side of the quilt.

The Quilting

Layer the quilt top with batting and backing.

Now it's time for the fun— the quilting!

He Says, She Says was made using gender-neutral colors. But after establishing the story of the quilt— half for him and half for her—it was easy to decide to quilt half of it with masculine-type quilting designs and the other half with flowery, more feminine designs.

Though this quilt is quilted as two distinct halves, I didn't want that to distract the viewer from the quilt top as a whole. I used matching thread and designs that were harmonious with one another. Of course, if you wanted to go all out, you could take it even further by using different colors of thread and more extreme designs.

The Feminine Side

Not many designs are more feminine than large, curvy feathers. To help the feather motif stand out, I quilted a dense back-and-forth design around it. The rest of the right side is quilted with additional swirly designs, such as feathers and faux ropes.

The Masculine Side

I continued my quilting by stitching masculine-feeling designs onto the left side of the quilt. Though I used a swirl pattern, a more geometric design would work equally well. Consider straight lines or squared designs, for example. I alternated some pointy designs—such as the plume feather—with straight lines.

Finishing

After you have completed the quilting, use your favorite method to attach the binding.

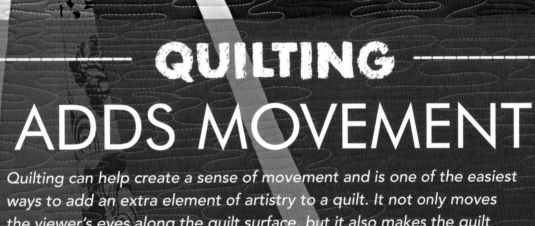

QUILTING
ADDS MOVEMENT

Quilting can help create a sense of movement and is one of the easiest ways to add an extra element of artistry to a quilt. It not only moves the viewer's eyes along the quilt surface, but it also makes the quilt more dynamic and interesting.

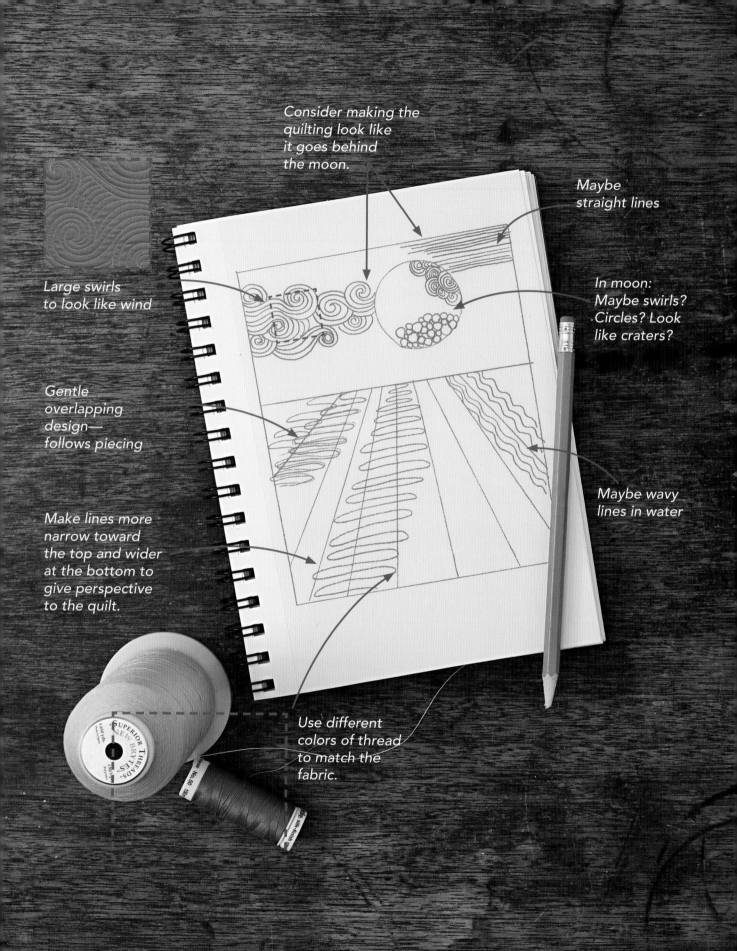

Consider making the
quilting look like
it goes behind
the moon.

Maybe
straight lines

Large swirls
to look like wind

In moon:
Maybe swirls?
Circles? Look
like craters?

Gentle
overlapping
design—
follows piecing

Maybe wavy
lines in water

Make lines more
narrow toward
the top and wider
at the bottom to
give perspective
to the quilt.

Use different
colors of thread
to match the
fabric.

Realistic Movement

If you have a recognizable image on your quilt top, such as a car or a kite, using quilting to add movement will make it look even more realistic. To make a car look like it is moving across the quilt, for example, add swirls to suggest smoke or wind behind the car. A kite that is flying high would need wind, so stitch swirls to represent the wind.

Don't feel as though you have to make every part of a quilt look as though it's moving. Consider adding just a little movement to a part of the quilt. The *Shooting Stars* quilt, below, has four stars—but to make just one of them look like a shooting star, I added some wavy lines from the star in the upper right to the edge of the quilt. This helps give the appearance of movement without being overwhelming.

Pieced and quilted by Angela Walters

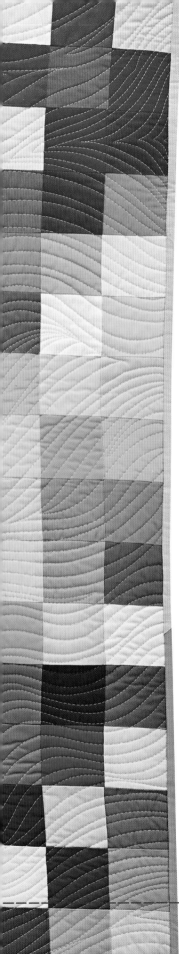

Other Kinds of Movement

Sometimes you may want to use quilting to add movement to a quilt that is more abstract. In *Megapixel*, at left, the colors flow in a wavy pattern. I knew that quilting an allover design wouldn't help emphasize the quilt's movement. Instead, I quilted lines that loosely followed the flow of the colors.

First I drew a few guidelines on the quilt to mark how I thought the colors flowed. Then I echo-quilted these lines again and again. In areas where the stitching intersected, I simply filled in with more lines, echoing the top and bottom areas.

Choosing the Right Designs

When choosing quilting designs, remember that any kind of design that moves the viewer's eye across the quilt will work for adding movement—swirly designs, wavy lines, and even straight lines. Experiment with different designs and different ways to use them.

Designed and pieced
by Emily Cier

Moonrise

FINISHED SIZE: 44½˝ × 60½˝

Pieced and machine quilted by Angela Walters

A quilt designed just for adding movement with the quilting? Yes, please! Unlike the bright colors of a sunrise, I wanted to use the darker, more muted colors of nighttime. Mix in quilting designs that add movement, and you have a quilt that is perfect for nighttime snuggling!

MATERIALS

Dark gray (for sky): 24½˝ × 44½˝

White or very light gray (for moon): 1 fat quarter

Various shades of blue, gray, and/or purple (for water): approximately ½ yard each

Binding: ½ yard

Backing: 3 yards

Batting: 52˝ × 68˝

Freezer paper: 36˝ × 44˝ (tape pieces together to make a piece that is large enough)

Water-soluble marker or chalk pencil

Large circular object (such as a bowl) to use as a pattern

Fusible interfacing

Making the Water Templates

1. Using a pen and ruler, draw lines radiating out from a side of the top edge of the freezer-paper template across to the bottom and side edges. This will be the water.

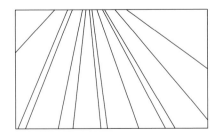

2. In numerical order, label the tops of the freezer-paper sections formed by the lines you have drawn. Assign each section a color, and mark the freezer paper accordingly. Carefully cut the paper on the lines to make the water templates.

3. Iron each piece of freezer paper to the *wrong* side of a blue, gray, or purple fabric piece, according to your markings.

4. Adding a ¼˝ seam allowance as you go, cut out each template shape using a rotary cutter and ruler.

tip *Refer to the Lava Lamp quilt (page 36) for illustrations showing how to make freezer-paper templates.*

Assembling the Quilt Top

1. With right sides together, line up the top edges of the first 2 numbered fabric sections. Sew together along the shared long edge, using a ¼˝ seam allowance.

2. Continue aligning the top edges and sewing the successive template shapes together until all the pieces have been joined.

3. Remove the freezer paper. If necessary, trim the edges to square up the quilt top.

tip *If you remove the freezer-paper templates carefully, you will be able to use them again!*

4. Sew the 24½˝ × 44½˝ dark gray sky piece to the top of the pieced water section.

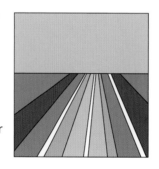

5. To make the moon, draw around the circular object onto the white fabric. Cut out the circle.

6. Following the manufacturer's directions, use fusible interfacing to fuse the moon circle onto the sky piece. Sew along the edges of the moon to secure it to the quilt top.

NOTE: *I wait until after I've sewn the two sections together to fuse on the moon so that I can position it perfectly, exactly where I want it.*

The Quilting

Layer the quilt top with batting and backing.

One of my favorite things to quilt is "water," so I designed a quilt that features a lot of it! Every design used in the quilting was planned to emphasize movement, from the wind in the sky to the waves in the water.

Quilting the Sky

In the sky portion, I quilted wavy lines to represent wind. Elongated swirls that look as if they overlap can suggest wind, water, or even hair! To ensure that the quilting would be visible for illustration purposes, I used a thread color slightly lighter than the quilt top, but thread that matches exactly would actually be best for this design.

To quilt the moon, several design options are available. Circles to look like craters or a large swirl would really make the moon shine on this quilt!

The long swirls in the sky suggest the movement of wind.

Quilting the Water

When quilting the water portion of this quilt, I used several different colors of thread. I chose threads that blended with each fabric color. The gentle back-and-forth quilting design starts out narrow at the top of the quilt and becomes wider at the bottom.

Even though I matched the thread to the quilt top, I purposely avoided staying within each color strip, instead allowing the quilting to overlap into the other sections. I think it looks like the water is overlapping—much as it would in real life.

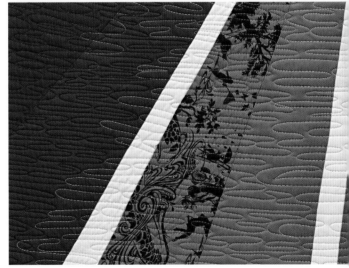

To indicate moving water, I quilted a back-and-forth design.

Finishing

Piece together the backing sections, and from the leftovers cut 2¼˝-wide binding strips—you will need about 6½ yards of binding. After you have completed the quilting, use your favorite method to attach the binding.

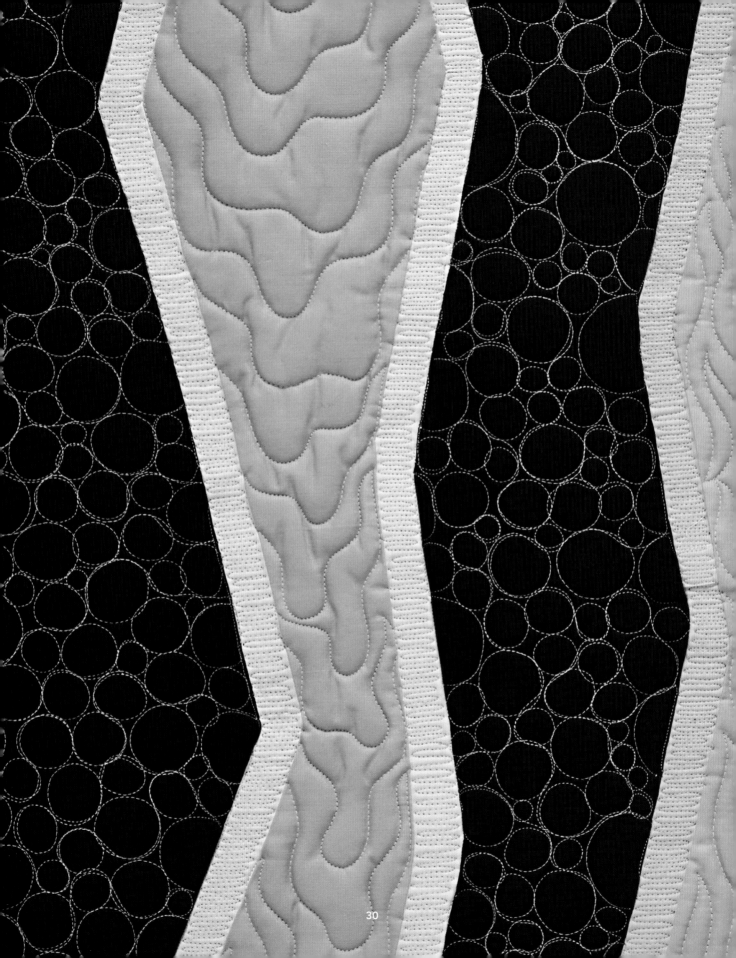

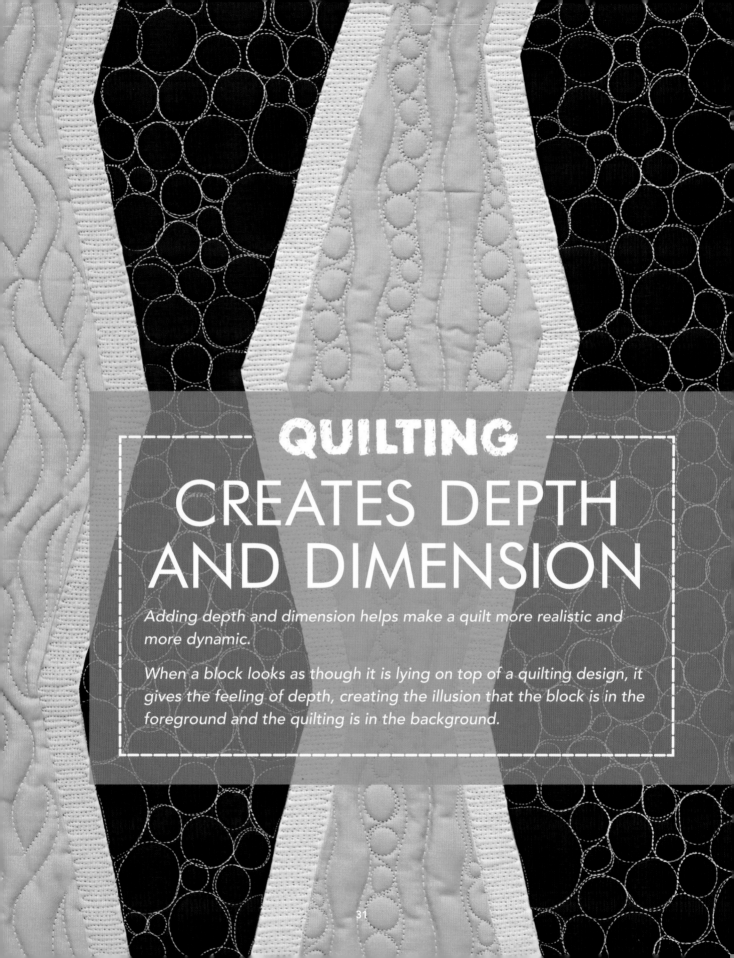

QUILTING
CREATES DEPTH AND DIMENSION

Adding depth and dimension helps make a quilt more realistic and more dynamic.

When a block looks as though it is lying on top of a quilting design, it gives the feeling of depth, creating the illusion that the block is in the foreground and the quilting is in the background.

Loose wavy lines to add movement

Maybe a figure-eight design in the yellow strip?

Wavy lines combined with pebbles also add movement.

Make the background design look like it goes behind the yellow strips.

Could also use swirls in background to add a sense of depth

Dense back-and-forth design in thin yellow strips

Leave thin strips unquilted to add a little definition?

Traveling to Add Depth

To make designs look as if they extend behind parts of a quilt, you need to travel. Traveling is simply stitching along a seam or other part of the quilt to move to a different area. Another benefit of traveling is that it allows you to keep the quilting designs the same size, rather than trying to squeeze in a complete design between sections.

In the quilt shown below, the quilted circles look as though they are going behind a block. When quilting around the blocks, I quilted half-circles that touched the block. Then I traveled along the block to start the next design.

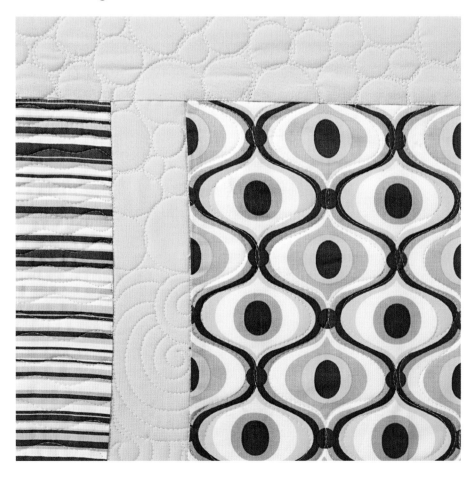

Seeing Squares is a great example of the use of this technique. I quilted wavy lines across the entire quilt except for a few squares. When I got to a square that I wanted to appear to be floating on top of the quilt, I traveled along the seam for approximately ½˝ and then stitched back in the opposite direction. This makes the quilting seem to go behind the square. As a result, a few portions of the quilt top really pop out, adding interest to the whole com-position. It isn't hard to do and actually makes for quick quilting!

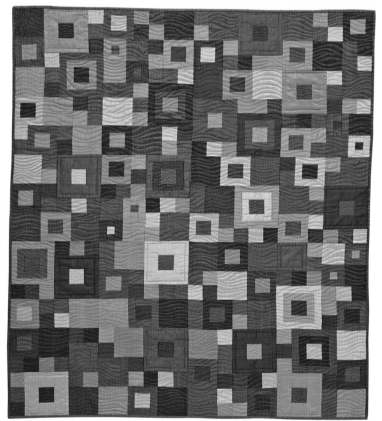

Designed and pieced by Shea Henderson

Adding Depth within Blocks

You don't necessarily have to make the quilting look as if it's going behind a block to add depth to a quilt. In the example of the carpenter block at right, I used quilting to make some parts seem to go under other portions *within* the block itself.

Quilting the block was as easy as quilting the same back-and-forth design, just going in different directions. I tried to imagine what the pieces would look like if they were woven together. The result is a look of depth within the block.

Pieced by Georgieanna Martin

Carpenter block: Look for ways to add depth within a block.

Some quilting designs, such as concentric circles and tiles, already look as if they are lying on top of one another. They give the illusion of depth all on their own. Try using them in background areas to help add depth to a quilt.

Lava Lamp

FINISHED SIZE: 28½˝ × 32½˝

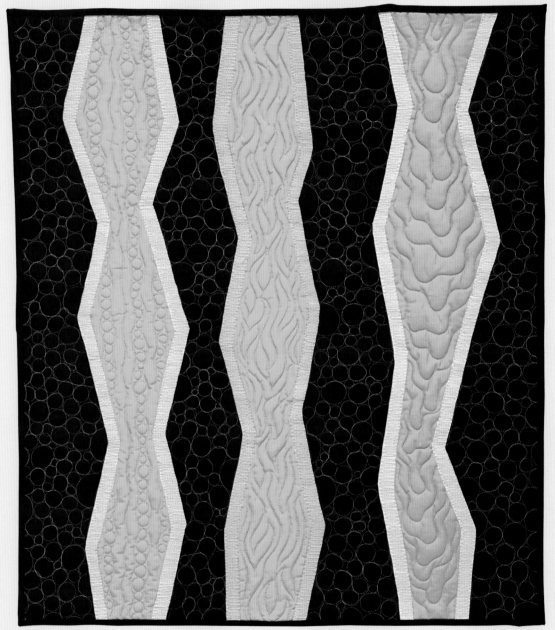

Pieced and machine quilted by Angela Walters

This fun and groovy project is made using templates drawn on freezer paper. Freezer paper is awesome because once it's ironed to the fabric, it stays put. But the templates are reusable and repositionable. This is definitely one of my favorite ways to make a quilt!

MATERIALS

Roll of freezer paper

Long ruler

Pencil or pen

Brown fabric for background and binding: 1⅛ yards

Light yellow fabric for lava: ⅜ yard

Orange fabric for lava: ⅝ yard

Backing: 1 yard

Batting: 35″ × 39″

Making the Templates

NOTE: *To make templates for the shapes in this wallhanging, first tape together freezer paper to make a 28″ × 32″ piece. If you want a bigger quilt, tape pieces of freezer paper together until you have the desired size. Be sure to put the tape on the matte, or paper, side of the freezer paper.*

1. Using a ruler, draw straight lines that pivot randomly down the freezer-paper template.

I drew 6 lines to form 3 orange sections. Then I went back and drew additional lines ½″ outside of each orange section to create the yellow strips.

There is no right way or wrong way to do this—do what you think looks good. Just remember that the more lines you draw, the more pieces you will need to cut.

tip *When marking the pivot points, keep in mind that the more extreme the angle, the trickier it will be to piece. If you are a beginner, consider making gentle turns.*

2. Label the top of each section, in sequence, with a number and the fabric color. This will help keep you organized when sewing the sections together.

tip *Even though I number my template pieces, I still use a camera to take a picture of the freezer paper before I cut it apart—just in case I get confused somewhere along the line.*

3. Carefully cut the template pieces apart on the lines.

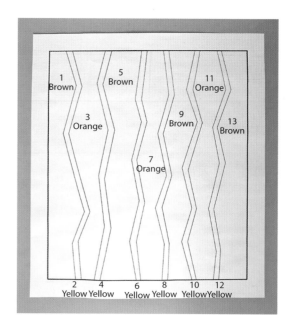

Cutting the Quilt Pieces

1. Organize the template pieces by fabric color. Carefully lay each template shape on the *wrong* side of the fabric, shiny side down, and iron it to the fabric using a low heat setting.

tip *If you are using a directional fabric, lay the template on the fabric so that the bottom (or top) edge runs parallel to the selvage. This could require more fabric, depending on your design, but the effect is worth it.*

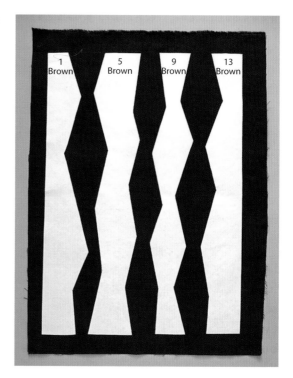

2. Using a rotary cutter and a ruler, cut out the fabric shape, adding a ¼˝ seam allowance as you cut. You may need scissors to reach into the angles.

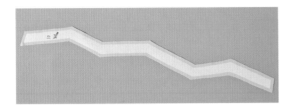

3. Cut out the rest of the shapes, continuing to add a ¼˝ seam allowance as you cut. *Do not take the freezer paper off!* Keeping it on will make it easier to sew the pieces together.

After all the pieces are cut out, place them in the order in which they are to be sewn together.

Assembling the Quilt Top

Sewing the zigzag strips together is easier than it might look. They can actually be sewn without using pins and without breaking up the stitching.

1. To join the strips, you are going to sew the seam in segments. The straight line between each pair of pivot points is a segment. Starting with the first 2 pieces, line up the first segment.

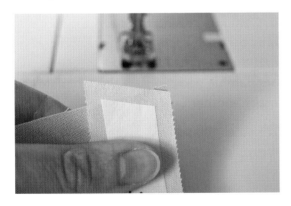

NOTE: *The rest of the strip won't match up when you line up the first segment, but don't worry about that. All you are focusing on right now is the first segment.*

2. Using a ¼˝ seam allowance, sew the strips together along the first segment. Stitch as close to the freezer paper as you can without actually sewing on it. Stop when you are at the pivot point— the point where the next segment starts.

tip *Marking the pivot point with a dot will help you to know where to stop stitching.*

3. Leaving the needle in the down position, lift the presser foot. Slightly lift the top fabric strip and carefully rotate the bottom strip so the next segment is lined

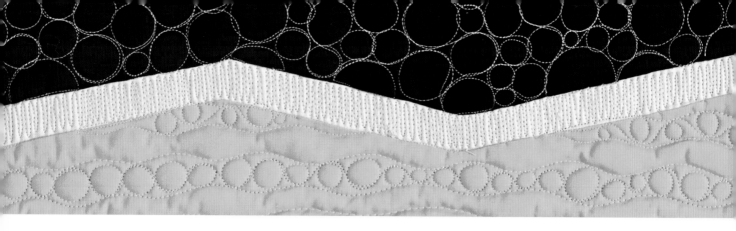

up to sew. The needle is still in the down position, so be careful not to pull too hard.

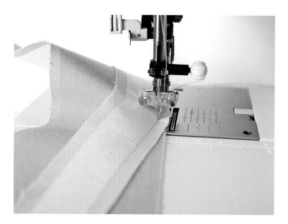

4. Rotate the top strip so that it lines up with the bottom strip. Lower the presser foot to hold the strips in place and check that the edges line up.

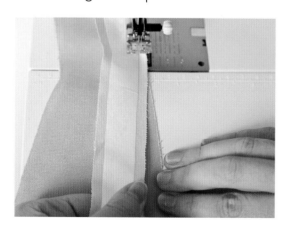

5. Sew the segment, stopping when you get to the next pivot point. Repeat until the strips are completely sewn together.

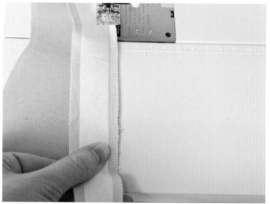

NOTE: *I leave the freezer paper on until the very end. This not only helps to keep the pieces organized, but it also helps to stabilize them during the sewing process.*

6. Continue sewing the strips together until the quilt top is completely pieced, and then remove the freezer paper. If you are careful, you can save the templates to make another quilt.

7. Iron all the seam allowances away from the yellow fabric.

The Quilting

Layer the quilt top with batting and backing.

The only thing more fun than making the *Lava Lamp* quilt top is quilting it. Get in a groovy mood and start quilting!

Quilting the Background

To establish the brown fabric as the background in this quilt, I wanted a lot of dense quilting on the brown sections. I chose to use bubble quilting, not only to help squish down the background but also to give the look of bubbles in a lava lamp.

To add depth, I quilted the bubbles to look as though they continue behind the orange and yellow pieces, adding to the feeling of depth in the quilt.

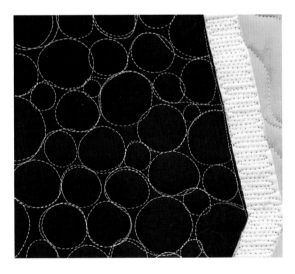

Quilting the Orange Sections

I wanted the orange parts of the quilt top to look like blobs of lava floating in a lava lamp, so I used designs that were flowy and less dense than the background stitching. In one of the orange sections, I quilted vertical wavy lines. To add more interest, I filled in between some of the wavy lines with small circles.

In the yellow strips, I quilted dense back-and-forth lines. I wanted this quilting to separate the orange and brown sections. It defines the orange and yellow sections without taking attention away from the quilt top as a whole.

Finishing

After you have completed the quilting, use your favorite method to attach the binding.

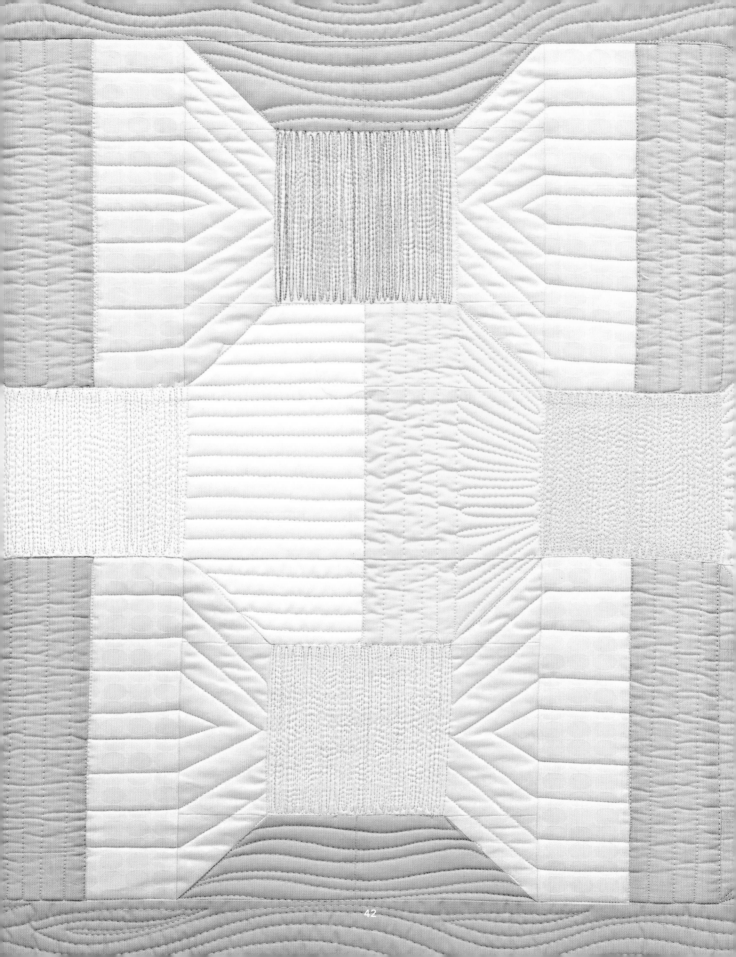

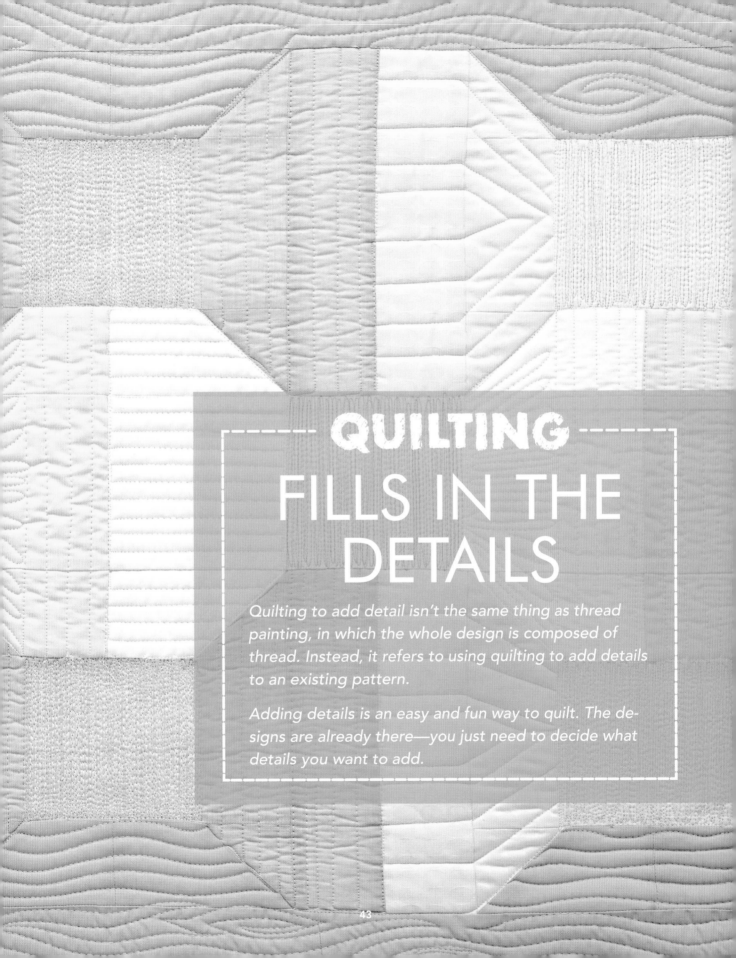

QUILTING
FILLS IN THE DETAILS

Quilting to add detail isn't the same thing as thread painting, in which the whole design is composed of thread. Instead, it refers to using quilting to add details to an existing pattern.

Adding details is an easy and fun way to quilt. The designs are already there—you just need to decide what details you want to add.

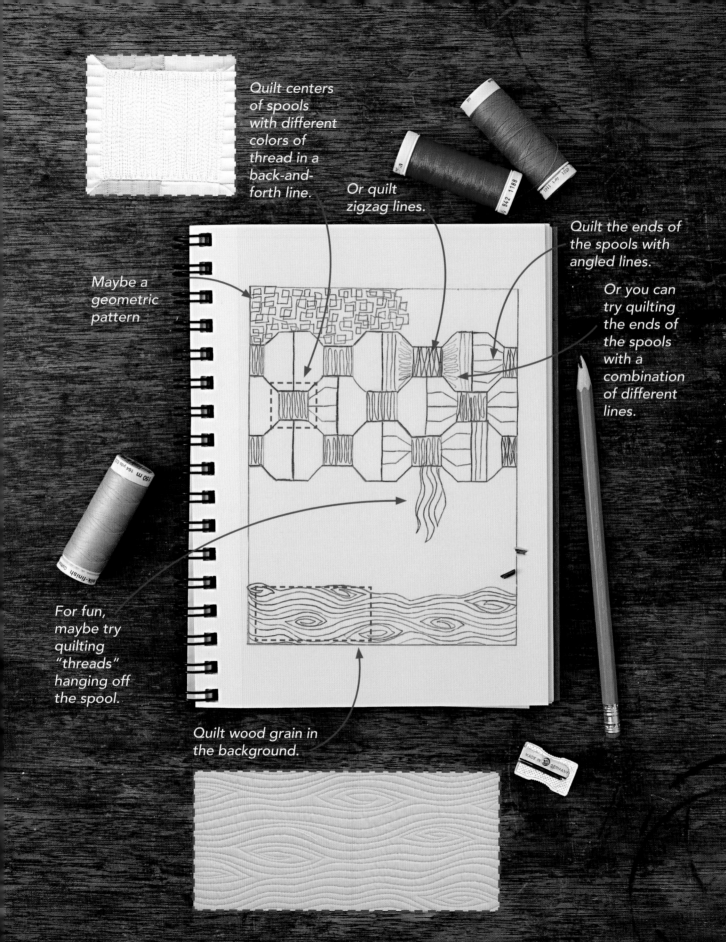

Quilt centers of spools with different colors of thread in a back-and-forth line.

Or quilt zigzag lines.

Quilt the ends of the spools with angled lines.

Or you can try quilting the ends of the spools with a combination of different lines.

Maybe a geometric pattern

For fun, maybe try quilting "threads" hanging off the spool.

Quilt wood grain in the background.

It's All in the Details

Quilting isn't just for holding a quilt together; it's for doing so much more to enhance the quilt. It can add a bit of realism to a quilt and make the whole quilting process more fun.

The details don't have to be obvious, or even noticeable. They can be something that's only noticeable upon closer inspection. You don't want to become so focused on quilting the details that you lose track of the rest of the quilt. Just do what comes easily and naturally, and then move on.

Details Change the Look of a Quilt

Sometimes adding details can change the look of the quilt altogether. For instance, if a quilt top features circles, you might add petals to make them look like flowers. Or perhaps you want to quilt the circles to look like suns, so you add sunrays with your quilting. The trick is not to limit your imagination but to have fun with it.

Details Help Define the Pattern

Sometimes adding quilting detail can define the pattern of the quilt and make it more noticeable.

In the *Quilt* quilt below, using a mod alphabet pattern to spell out the word *quilt* creates an abstract-looking design. But to help show that the blocks are actually letters and not just random blocks, I quilted the letter in the center of each block. Adding the details helps make the pattern easier to see.

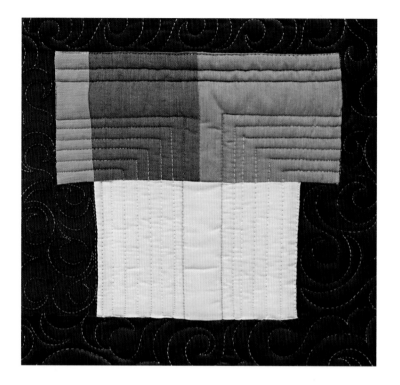

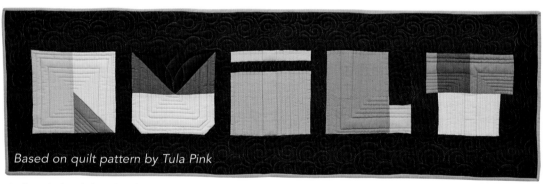

Based on quilt pattern by Tula Pink

Quilting helps define the abstract letters.

Details Make It More Realistic

On a quilt that depicts an object—such as a flower or a tree—adding quilting details can make that object look more realistic. Coming up with quilting ideas is as easy as paying attention to how things look in real life.

The amount of detail that you can add is endless. For the house block sample above, I stitched in all the details that I could think of—shingles in the roof, picket fences in the background, windows on the house, flowers and trees in the background, and lots more.

Spools

FINISHED SIZE: 54½˝ × 60½˝ • **Finished block size: 8˝ × 12˝**

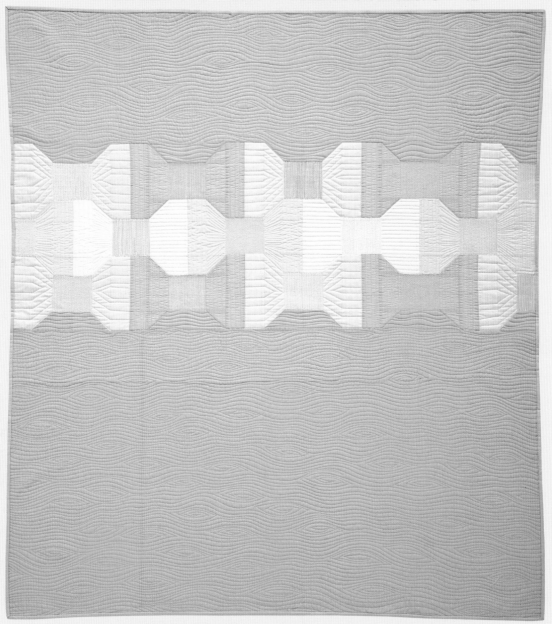

Pieced by Kathy Limpic and machine quilted by Angela Walters

It's no secret that I am addicted to thread, so a quilt design that resembles vintage spools of thread was just a given. This quilt makes a great practice piece for beginners and a quick project for more experienced quilters.

MATERIALS

Tan (for background and binding): 2½ yards of fabric with usable width of at least 42″

Cream (for spools): ¾ yard

Green (for spools): ½ yard

Yellow (for spools): ⅜ yard

White (for spools): ⅓ yard

Backing: 3⅝ yards

Batting: 62″ × 68″

CUTTING

Tan

Cut 1 rectangle 10½″ × 54½″.

Cut 1 rectangle 30½″ × 54½″.

Cut 2 strips 2½″ × width of fabric; subcut into 18 rectangles 2½″ × 4½″.

Cut 7 strips 2¼″ × width of fabric for binding.

Cream

Cut 20 squares 2½″ × 2½″.

Cut 4 rectangles 4½″ × 8½″.

Cut 10 rectangles 2½″ × 8½″.

Cut 2 squares 4½″ × 4½″.

Green

Cut 4 rectangles 4½″ × 8½″.

Cut 8 rectangles 2½″ × 8½″.

Cut 16 squares 2½″ × 2½″.

Yellow

Cut 10 rectangles 2½″ × 4½″.

Cut 1 rectangle 4½″ × 6½″.

Cut 2 rectangles 4½″ × 12½″.

White

Cut 2 rectangles 4½″ × 12½″.

Cut 8 rectangles 2½″ × 4½″.

Making the Blocks

1. With right sides together, lay a 2½″ × 2½″ square on a 2½″ × 4½″ rectangle, aligning them at an end. Sew a line diagonally from the top right to the bottom left of the square.

tip *Quick corner triangles are made by sewing squares at the corners of larger rectangles. In this project they form the angled edges of the spools. Before trimming away the corner, you can use the base rectangle to check that the corner is square.*

2. Trim away the corner above the stitching, leaving a ¼″ seam allowance. Press open.

3. Repeat the steps so that you end up with all the following combinations:

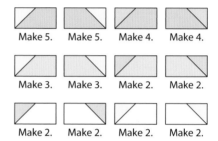

Make 5.   Make 5.   Make 4.   Make 4.

Make 3.   Make 3.   Make 2.   Make 2.

Make 2.   Make 2.   Make 2.   Make 2.

Assembling the Rows

The First Row

1. Piece 2 blocks according to the diagram below.

2. Piece 2 blocks as shown in the diagram below.

3. Sew a half-block following the diagram below.

4. Starting with a unit from Step 1, sew the blocks together end to end to form a row, alternating between the 2 different block colors. Finish the row with the half-block.

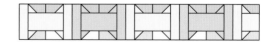

The Second Row

To assemble the second pieced row, sew the 4½″ × 6½″ yellow rectangle with the 4½″ × 12½″ white and yellow rectangles, alternating colors as shown.

The Third Row

1. Piece 2 of each of the blocks below. These blocks are mirror images of the blocks in the first row.

2. Piece a half-block as shown below—a mirror image of the half-block in the first row.

3. Sew the blocks and half-block together to form a strip as shown.

Assembling the Quilt Top

1. Sew the 3 rows together as shown in the assembly diagram to form the pieced section of the quilt.

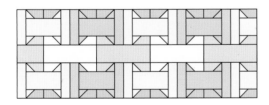

2. To complete the quilt top, sew the 10½″ × 54½″ background fabric strip to the top of the pieced section. Sew the 30½″ × 54½″ background fabric strip to the bottom of the pieced section.

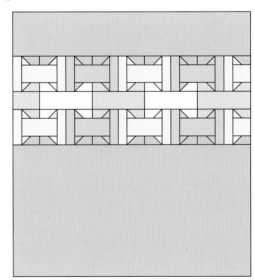

The Quilting

Layer the quilt top with batting and backing.

Because I envisioned the interlocking blocks as spools of thread, I knew I wanted to quilt them to look like that. My own thread rack is filled with all sorts of fun colors, so I decided to quilt the spools in bright colors. I quilted lines to look like thread across the middle part of each spool.

When I get going on a quilting theme, I have a hard time veering away from it! So when it came time to choose the quilting design for the background of this quilt, I went with a wood-grain design reminiscent of my wooden thread holder.

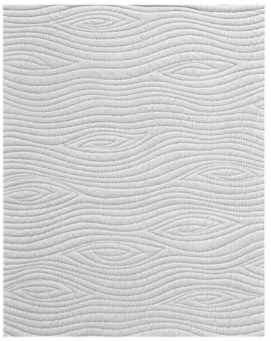

Background quilting

Of course, this quilt doesn't have to be quilted to look like spools of thread—that's just one suggestion. Try other techniques to make a quilt that is truly unique.

Finishing

After you have completed the quilting, use your favorite method to attach the binding.

Quilting fills the spools with thread.

QUILTING
PUTS THE FOCUS ON THE PIECING

Stitching in-the-ditch is a technique often hated by quilters, but it is so important as a way to emphasize the piecing! With some mild persuasion and plenty of tips, I hope to have you convinced that stitching in-the-ditch can be (almost) fun!

I remember when I was first learning how to stitch in-the-ditch. After a few attempts, I was left with lines that went all over the place. As I was ripping out the stitching and cursing under my breath, my husband came over and surveyed my not-so-great workmanship. "Maybe you should just stick with meandering," he said.

Talk about a challenge (and a hit to my pride)! It took me a while, but I finally did learn how to stitch in-the-ditch, and now I really like doing it.

Quilters tend to fall into two groups—those who never stitch in-the-ditch, and those who only stitch in-the-ditch. But I think that great quilting needs both stitching in-the-ditch and quilting designs.

In the background use random vertical and horizontal lines.

Maybe wavy lines

Or quilt densely with alternating designs.

Maybe a round design to contrast with straight lines

Pick designs that work well in skinny strips.

Leave alternate strips unquilted or quilt just a single line.

NOTE: *I think of stitching in-the-ditch kind of the way I think about waxed eyebrows. No one really notices them, but they do make the whole face look polished!*

Why Stitch in-the-Ditch?

What's the point of quilting in-the-ditch if no one is going to see it anyway? I am so glad you asked! Stitching along the seamlines stabilizes a quilt and keeps the seams straight and even. It also makes the quilt lie nice and flat.

Different quilters have different approaches to stitching in-the-ditch. I like to stitch in-the-ditch around the quilting area first and then fill it in with my quilting designs, whereas others like to quilt the designs first and then stitch around the seams. In my opinion, the order doesn't matter, as long as you *do* it.

Getting in-the-Ditch

When stitching in-the-ditch, it sure does help to have a "ditch" to stitch in. The ditch is formed when the seam allowance is carefully pressed to one side, creating a high side and a low side. You will quilt along the low side—the side without the seam allowances. Quilting in-the-ditch makes the low side a little lower, so that the high side overhangs the low side and the stitches will be almost hidden.

A well-ironed seam is the key to success.

Pressing correctly will help you out immensely down the line. When you are quilting along the seam, the difference between the higher and lower sides will make it easier to stay in-the-ditch.

A seam that isn't pressed properly makes stitching in-the-ditch harder because the bulk of the fabric will fall right under the stitching.

What about Pressing the Seam Open?

There are two sides to every discussion, and this one is no different. Some quilters prefer to press their seams open, which does help the quilt to lie flat. But in my experience, it's easier to stitch in the seam when there's a low area. Also, if you iron the seam open and then quilt along the seam, you will be stitching only on thread.

But this is just my opinion. Do whatever works best for you!

When to Stitch in-the-Ditch

The good news is that you don't have to stitch in every seam of a quilt top. Most often, I only stitch in-the-ditch around areas that repeat the same quilting design.

For instance, when quilting the block in the photograph below, made up of several small squares, I didn't stitch around every seam. I only stitched in-the-ditch around the white squares that were quilted with a design different from all the others. Since the rest of the squares were quilted with the same swirl design, I didn't stitch along those seams.

Tips for Great Stitching in-the-Ditch

As with any other quilting technique, practice is the key to near-perfection. But a few tips will make it easier.

- **Use matching thread.** Using thread that matches the fabric will help ensure that every little bump and bobble won't be obvious. If the fabrics are different colors, try to pick a thread that blends with both of them.

- **Get friendly with your iron.** A properly ironed seam will make stitching in-the-ditch much easier. Using a spray starch such as Mary Ellen's Best Press will help the seams lie as flat as possible.

- **Don't be too tough on yourself.** When you are machine quilting, your nose is inches away from the quilt. Every little mistake is noticeable. Once you are actually using the quilt, though, chances are you won't even see the mistakes.

- **Take a break.** Precision quilting is like pitching in the major leagues. Every once in a while you will have an off day. If you aren't feeling in the groove, move on to a different area and come back later.

- **Relax!** No matter how good you are at machine quilting, if you are tense, it's going to show in your quilting. Keep your shoulders relaxed and loose. Not only will your body thank you, but your quilting will look better, too!

- **Use a good ruler.** For longarm quilters, a good ruler will make all the difference when it comes to stitching in-the-ditch. And when I say a good ruler, I'm talking about one that works for *you*. Some people like a thin ruler, and some like a short ruler. Experiment until you find what works for you. I have found that a longer, thinner ruler works best for me.

Dead End

FINISHED SIZE: 40½˝ × 51½˝

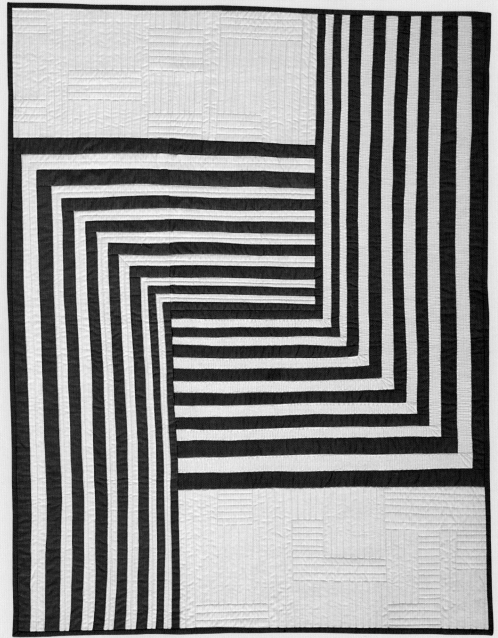

Pieced and machine quilted by Angela Walters

This wallhanging will give you lots of chances to work on your stitch-in-the-ditch quilting. By the time you have finished *Dead End*, you'll have it down pat. It takes a little practice, but it will make the piecing shine! Before you can practice your quilting, though, you first need to make the quilt.

MATERIALS

Cream solid (for background): 1¾ yards

Blue solid (for stripes): ¾ yard

Gray solid (for stripes): ¾ yard

Backing and binding: 2½ yards

Batting: 48″ × 58″

CUTTING

Cream

Cut 5 strips 1¼″ × width of fabric.

Cut 9 strips 1½″ × width of fabric.

Cut 7 strips 1¾″ × width of fabric.

Cut rectangles 11½″ × 25½″, 9½″ × 15½″, and 9½″ × 10½″.

Blue

Cut 2 strips 1¼″ × width of fabric.

Cut 6 strips 1½″ × width of fabric.

Cut 4 strips 1¾″ × width of fabric.

Gray

Cut 2 strips 1¼″ × width of fabric.

Cut 6 strips 1½″ × width of fabric.

Cut 4 strips 1¾″ × width of fabric.

Making the Quilt Top

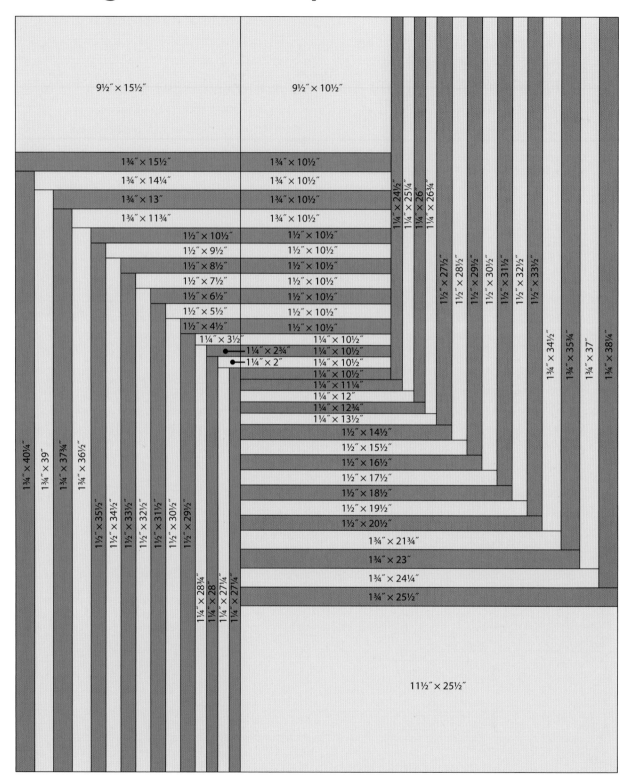

9½" × 15½"

9½" × 10½"

1¾" × 15½"

1¾" × 10½"

1¾" × 14¼"

1¾" × 10½"

1¾" × 13"

1¾" × 10½"

1¾" × 11¾"

1¾" × 10½"

1¼" × 24½"

1¼" × 25¼"

1¼" × 26"

1¼" × 26¾"

1½" × 10½"

1½" × 10½"

1½" × 9½"

1½" × 10½"

1½" × 8½"

1½" × 10½"

1½" × 7½"

1½" × 10½"

1½" × 6½"

1½" × 10½"

1½" × 5½"

1½" × 10½"

1½" × 4½"

1½" × 10½"

1½" × 27½"

1½" × 28½"

1½" × 29½"

1½" × 30½"

1½" × 31½"

1½" × 32½"

1½" × 33½"

1¼" × 3½"

1¼" × 2¾"

1¼" × 2"

1¼" × 10½"

1¼" × 10½"

1¼" × 10½"

1¼" × 10½"

1¼" × 11¼"

1¼" × 12"

1¼" × 12¾"

1¼" × 13½"

1¾" × 34½"

1¾" × 35¾"

1¾" × 37"

1¾" × 38¼"

1½" × 14½"

1½" × 15½"

1½" × 16½"

1½" × 17½"

1½" × 18½"

1½" × 19½"

1½" × 20½"

1¾" × 21¾"

1¾" × 23"

1¾" × 24¼"

1¾" × 25½"

1¾" × 40¼"

1¾" × 39"

1¾" × 37¾"

1¾" × 36½"

1½" × 35½"

1½" × 34½"

1½" × 33½"

1½" × 32½"

1½" × 31½"

1½" × 30½"

1½" × 29½"

1¼" × 28¾"

1¼" × 28"

1¼" × 27¼"

1¼" × 27¼"

11½" × 25½"

1. Referring to the strip sizes and colors in the diagram on page 62, cut 2 blue and 2 cream strips 1¼″ × 10½″. Sew strips along their long edges, alternating colors.

tip *Because all the strips are different sizes, I simply cut them as I go. It may be tempting to just sew on pieces and then cut them to the right size, but measuring each one will ensure that the quilt top ends up square.*

2. Sew the next 7 strips (4 blue and 3 cream), alternating the colors and using strip size 1½″ × 10½″.

3. Sew the next 4 strips (2 blue and 2 cream), alternating the colors and using strip size 1¾″ × 10½″.

4. Sew the 9½″ × 10½″ cream rectangle to the top of the unit from Step 3.

NOTE: *Be sure to press each seam carefully with a warm iron. If you use an iron that is too hot or if you press too hard, the strips will become distorted.*

5. As shown below, sew a 1¼″ × 24¼″ gray strip along the right-hand side of the block. Sew a 1¼″ × 11¼″ gray strip to the bottom of the block.

6. Using the strip sizes and colors indicated in the diagram, continue sewing on pieces until all the strips (8 gray and 7 cream, to the right and to the bottom) have been stitched in place.

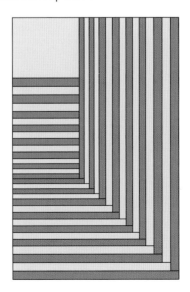

7. Sew an 11½″ × 25½″ cream rectangle to the bottom of the block.
Set aside.

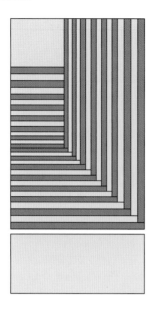

8. Now begin piecing the second
side. Matching long sides, sew
a 1¼″ × 27¼″ blue strip to a
1¼″ × 27¼″ cream strip. Press.

9. Sew a 1¼″ × 2″ cream
rectangle to the top of the
pieced strips. Make sure the
blue strip is on the right.

10. Using the diagram at
right as a guide and the
diagram on page 62 to get
strip sizes, continue sewing
on strips, alternating colors
and switching between the top
and the side. Continue until all
the strips have been used.

11. Sew a 9½″ × 15½″ cream
rectangle to the top.

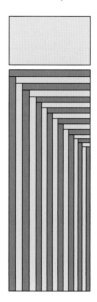

12. Matching up the strips, sew
the 2 pieced sections together to
form the quilt top. Trim the quilt if
necessary to square it up.

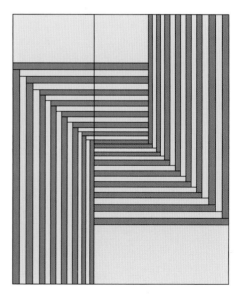

The Quilting

Layer the quilt top with batting and backing.

By this point in the chapter, you've probably guessed that the quilting of this piece involves stitching in-the-ditch. So get ready for some fun!

Quilting the Strip Section

I used matching thread and stitched along each of the seams before quilting any of the filler. This helps keep the seams as straight as they can be.

But as I've said earlier, a quilt usually needs more than just stitching in-the-ditch. I quilted straight lines between the blue strips. And for something a little different, I quilted dense back-and-forth lines between the gray strips.

I faced a little dilemma when it was time to quilt within the strips. I usually can't stand to leave any portion of a quilt untouched—I like to quilt my quilts to death. But this time I left the gray and blue strips unquilted. I like the way they stand out against the dense quilting on the cream strips.

Quilting the Background

I quilted more straight lines in the background portion of the quilt. But instead of doing the same old lines, I changed it up a bit.

I randomly quilted vertical and horizontal lines, making it up as I went along. This gave me even more practice with the ruler, and I ended up with an interesting design that complements the quilt top.

Finishing

Piece together the backing sections, and from the leftovers cut 2¼˝-wide binding strips—you will need about 5¾ yards of binding. After you have completed the quilting, use your favorite method to attach the binding.

QUILTING
MAKES THE QUILT

Sometimes the quilting wants to be more than just another layer of art or the last thought. Sometimes it wants to be the star of the quilt. In this chapter you'll learn how to take your quilting from the background to center stage and really make it shine.

Tiny filler between letters

Pick a big quilting design as an accent.

Leave area between bricks unquilted.

Small quilting around design makes it "pop."

Maybe all pebbles? Maybe switch to swirls?

Use a variety of designs in each letter.

Quilt bricks with straight lines or echo the blocks.

Try a geometric design.

Quilting as the Main Focus

Sometimes I just have to work backward! I like to come up with a quilting design and *then* make a quilt to fit the design. This shows off the quilting in all its glory. When the quilting is what makes the quilt, a lot more thought needs to go into the designs—no boring meanders here!

A Wholecloth Quilt with a Modern Twist

A traditional wholecloth quilt top is one that's made of a plain piece of fabric, usually white or light-colored, with the quilting being the focus and the only design. Wholecloth quilts date back to the 1800s and were considered works of art. Women would spend years making elaborate wholecloth quilts of this type.

Quilting a solid piece of fabric isn't the only option, of course. The quilting can still have the starring role if the quilt top is pieced. But to ensure that your quilting isn't upstaged, consider making a quilt top with minimal piecing or with fabrics that read as solids. This will ensure that your hard work will be seen!

Quilted by Jeanne Rumans

A traditional wholecloth quilt is quilted on a solid piece of fabric.

A Reversible Quilt

Some quilts are made with busy fabrics that don't show the quilting at all. Instead of just quilting an allover design, switch the quilt around. Quilt an intricate design that will show on the back. *Voilà!* You will have a two-sided quilt.

Quilt front

Quilt back

Making Your Quilting Show

Of course, if the quilting is going to be the star, you need to be able to see it! Consider the following factors to make sure that your hard work will be seen.

Choosing the Right Thread

Before you start quilting, you need to decide how prominent you want the quilting to be. You may want to use a thread that blends so that the design isn't glaring. If you want the quilting to be more visible, use thread that's a shade or two lighter or darker than the fabric. Be careful to not use thread that contrasts *too* much, or every bump and bobble in the quilting will be very visible!

To Puff or Not to Puff?

Consider using a batting with a higher loft to help show off your quilting. I'm not talking about a high-loft batting, but one that has just a little bit of puff to it. A puffier batting will help emphasize the difference between dense and less dense areas of quilting.

Sometimes I opt for two layers of batting instead of using a puffier batting. I like to use a thinner poly batting as the base and a batting with slightly higher loft on top. This adds a little more stiffness to the quilt, but it really makes the quilting pop!

NOTE: *I used two layers of Quilter's Dream Poly Select batting when I quilted my* Mod Wholecloth Quilt. *It helps make the letters stand out a little more.*

The Star of the Show: The Quilting Design

Now that the stage is set, you are ready to create the most important part of this quilt—the quilting design. It sounds more difficult than it really is. You have a number of options for coming up with designs.

Using a Stencil

If you need a little help choosing designs, or if you just want some inspiration, consider using stencils. Stencils are easy to mark and come in a range of designs. Just remember that with stencils, what you see is what you get; you can't easily make a stenciled design larger or smaller.

Look for continuous-line stencils or machine-quilting stencils. These have designs that can be quilted in a continuous line without starts or stops. There's nothing worse than marking your whole quilt, only to realize that the stencil is a hand-quilting stencil with numerous stopping points!

Creating Your Own Design

If you can't find exactly what you are looking for in a stencil, try making up your own design. Using a piece of freezer paper, draw a design using a dark marker. This will allow you to "trace" the design onto the quilt top over and over again. Alternatively, you can mark a design directly on the quilt top. Use whichever method is easier for you.

The design might be one of these:

■ A special word, name, or saying

■ A symbol that is meaningful to you—a peace sign or a heart, for example

■ A mixture of your favorite quilting designs

These are just ideas to help you get started. Don't limit your own imagination—the possibilities are endless!

NOTE: *I like to use freezer paper for drawing my quilting designs. It is thicker than standard drawing paper, so it will hold up to repeated use. And because it comes on a wide roll, you can cut off bigger pieces than the normal 8½˝ × 11˝ sheets.*

Transferring the Design

When you have decided on a design, you will need to mark it on the quilt. Marking a quilt takes a little time, but the result will be a design that looks exactly the way you want it to. Several methods can be used to mark the quilt.

Pounce Pads

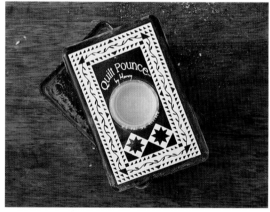

A pounce pad makes marking stencils quick and easy! A pounce pad looks similar to a chalkboard eraser, with loose chalk powder under a cloth-type

covering. When the pad is gently brushed over the stencil, the chalk marks the design lines on the quilt. Pounce pads come in white and blue (for white fabrics).

The chalk is easy to remove—just brush it off with your hand or lightly iron it. You do have to be careful when using a pounce pad. Because the chalk is so easily removed, moving the quilt top can make it come off. This can leave you without your road map.

tip *When using a pounce pad, lightly brush it over the stencil. Moving the pad too quickly or vigorously will result in sloppy lines and too much chalk.*

Water-Soluble Pens

I love using water-soluble markers and never have had any trouble removing the marks they make. These pens are great for marking stencils, drawing freehand designs, or tracing. The line can be as thick or as thin as you like and will stay put until you remove it with water.

The drawback to water-soluble pens is that you need to get the quilt wet to remove the marks, sometimes more than once. This can take away precious quilting time! Also, the marks won't show on busy prints or blue fabrics.

Chalk Pencils

Chalk pencils are another great option. Marks made with chalk pencils stay put longer than the chalk in a pounce pad, but using them with a stencil means a lot of sharpening. They come in several different colors, including blue, white, and pink. I especially like these when I need to mark quilts made with busy print fabrics on which my blue water-soluble pens won't show up.

tip *If you are quilting a design that should be centered on the quilt, it is very helpful to mark registration lines on the quilt top. Mark the center point of each side and draw lines to the center of the quilt to ensure that you are marking the design in the center of the quilt.*

Mod Wholecloth Quilt

FINISHED SIZE: 48½″ × 48½″

Pieced and machine quilted by Angela Walters

Now that you have all the tools, it's time to make a quilt that will be the stage to some awesome quilting! The *Mod Wholecloth Quilt* is a fun spin on a traditional wholecloth quilt. With just a bit of piecing to reinforce the theme of the quilt, there is plenty of room to let your quilting shine.

MATERIALS

Gray (for background): 2 yards

Taupe (for bricks): ⅓ yard (or scraps)

Backing and binding: 3¼ yards

Batting: 56″ × 56″

tip *Using sticky notes to label the various background sections will save you a lot of time when it comes to putting the quilt top together.*

CUTTING

Gray

Cut the following pieces for the rows:

9″ × 20″ (Row 1)

5½″ × 45½″ (Row 2)

15½″ × 48½″ (Row 3)

6½″ × 39″ (Row 4)

8½″ × 38½″ (Row 5)

3½″ × 6″ (Row 6a)

6″ × 32″ (Row 6b)

Cut

1 rectangle 2½″ × 7″

2 squares 3″ × 3″

4 rectangles 3″ × 3½″

2 rectangles 3″ × 4″

3 rectangles 3½″ × 4″

1 rectangle 3½″ × 6″

1 rectangle 3½″ × 9½″

2 rectangles 4″ × 7″

1 square 6½″ × 6½″

Cut 2 strips 1″ × width of fabric; subcut into

3 strips 1″ × 3″

1 strip 1″ × 3½″

1 strip 1″ × 7″

1 strip 1″ × 8½″

1 strip 1″ × 9½″

2 strips 1″ × 14″

Taupe

Cut 3 strips 3″ × width of fabric; subcut into

12 rectangles 3″ × 7″

4 rectangles 3″ × 3½″

Making the Quilt Top

To make the piecing easier to understand, this quilt pattern is divided into rows.

The First Row

1. Sew a 3″ × 7″ brick rectangle to each side of a 1″ × 3″ gray strip. Press. Sew a 1″ × 14″ gray strip to the top of the unit.

2. Sew a 3″ × 4″ gray rectangle to each side of a 3″ × 7″ brick. Press the seams toward the gray fabric.

3. Sew a 1″ × 14″ gray strip to connect the units from Step 1 and Step 2.

4. Sew a 6½″ × 6½″ gray square to the left side of the unit from Step 3. Press and set aside.

5. Sew a 3″ × 7″ brick to each side of a 1″ × 3″ gray strip. Sew a 3″ × 3½″ gray rectangle to the left-side brick. Sew a 3″ × 3½″ gray rectangle to the right-side brick.

6. Sew the units from Steps 4 and 5 together as shown. You should end up with a unit that measures 9″ × 20″. Press and set aside.

7. Sew a 3″ × 3″ gray square to the side of a 3″ × 7″ brick. Repeat to make a second unit.

8. Join the units from Step 7 with a 1″ × 9½″ gray strip.

9. Sew a 3½″ × 9½″ gray rectangle to the bottom of the unit from Step 8.

10. Use a 9″ × 20″ gray strip to join the units from Step 6 and Step 9. This will be the top row of the quilt.

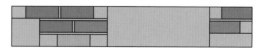

First row assembly

The Second Row

1. Sew a 3″ × 3½″ gray rectangle to a 3″ × 3½″ brick along the 3½″ side.

2. Sew a 5½″ × 45½″ gray strip to the left side of the unit, as shown.

Second row assembly

The Third Row

The 15½″ × 48½″ gray strip is the third row.

tip *If you are using scraps for the background fabric, sew pieces together until you have a strip that is 48½″ long.*

The Fourth Row

1. Sew a 3½″ × 4″ gray rectangle to a 3″ × 3½″ brick.

2. Sew a 4″ × 7″ gray rectangle to a 3″ × 7″ brick.

3. Sew the units from Step 1 and Step 2 to the ends of the 6½″ × 39″ gray strip.

Fourth row assembly

The Fifth Row

1. Sew a 1″ × 3½″ gray background rectangle between the longer sides of 2 bricks 3″ × 3½″. Sew a 3″ × 3½″ gray rectangle to the bottom of the unit.

2. Sew a 1″ × 8½″ gray strip to the left side of the unit from Step 1.

3. Sew a 2½″ × 7″ gray rectangle to the top of a 3″ × 7″ brick. Sew a 4″ × 7″ gray rectangle to the bottom of the brick. Sew this unit to the left side of the unit completed in Step 2.

4. Sew the 8½″ × 38½″ gray strip to the left side of the unit from Step 3.

Fifth row assembly

The Sixth Row

1. Sew a 1″ × 7″ gray strip to the top of a 3″ × 7″ brick. Sew a 3½″ × 4″ gray rectangle to each side of the unit.

2. Sew a 1″ × 3″ gray strip between 2 bricks 3″ × 7″.

3. Sew the Step 2 unit to the top of the Step 1 unit.

4. Sew a 3½″ × 6″ gray rectangle to the left side of the unit, and sew the 6″ × 32″ gray strip to the right side of the unit.

Sixth row assembly

Assembling the Quilt Top

Sew the 6 rows together according to the quilt top assembly diagram. Trim the edges to square up the quilt, if necessary.

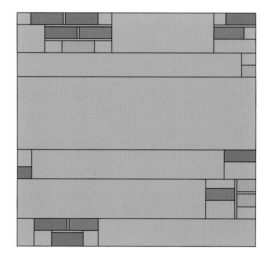

The Quilting

Layer the top, batting, and backing.

This quilt is a great example of designing a quilt backward—starting with an idea for a quilting design and then making a quilt around it. The quilting was inspired by graffiti that I saw on a train. The letters were so bright and vibrant that I just knew I wanted to re-create the same look on a quilt. The quilt top gives a hint of a brick wall, and the quilting forms the graffiti that adorns the wall.

Marking the Design

Once I decided on my word, *inspire*, I drew it on a sheet of paper. I tried to make it look a little like graffiti by scrunching the letters together and making them overlap. When I was happy with the way it looked, I took it to a print shop and had it enlarged to the size I wanted.

NOTE: *You could just draw your design larger and save yourself the time it takes to go to the print shop, but I find that drawing smaller is easier for me. Do whatever works for you!*

I don't have a lightbox, so I taped the paper to a window. Then I taped the quilt top over it. With the sun shining through, I was able to trace the design through the dark fabric of the quilt top.

I wanted the quilting for my *Mod Wholecloth Quilt* to achieve two goals: I wanted to reinforce the look of a brick wall, and I wanted to make the word *inspire* really stand out.

Quilting the Background

Within the individual "bricks," I quilted straight lines echoing from the outside toward the inside. I left the spaces between the bricks unquilted, to replicate the mortar.

In some places, I also quilted a bubble design to look as though it was spilling over the brick.

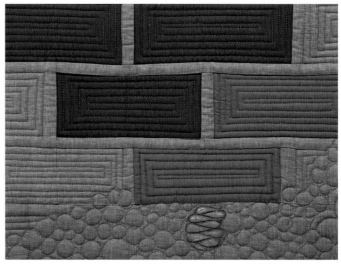

I wanted the quilting to reinforce the look of bricks.

Quilting the Letters

As I quilted around the letters in the word, I filled in each letter with a different quilting design. I knew that I would be painting the letters later with Shiva Paintstiks, so I wanted to add a lot of texture.

Around the letters, I densely quilted little circles. Because I was using two layers of batting, I knew the tiny quilting around the letters would make them pop out even more!

I stitched a different design in each of the letters.

Finishing

After you have completed the quilting, use your favorite method to attach the binding.

Embellishing the Quilt

I don't usually embellish my quilts, but I really, *really* wanted the quilting to accentuate the look of spray-painted graffiti. So after the quilt was quilted and bound, I painted the letters with Shiva Paintstiks. I love the way the paint makes the letters look like the graffiti that inspired the quilt in the first place.

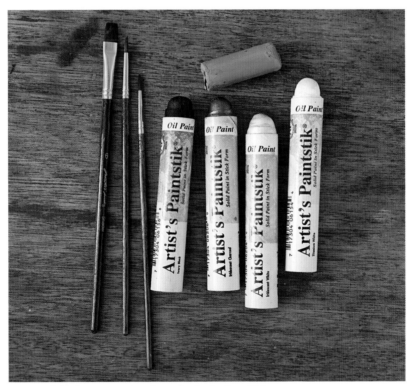

I painted the letters to give them the look of graffiti.

NOTE: *You don't have to paint the quilt as I did, of course. The quilted letters will still look great all on their own.*

QUILTING
PROVIDES
CONTRAST

Quilting can be a powerful tool. When used correctly, it can define a pattern and add contrast. But used incorrectly, it can detract from the quilt top. This chapter is the result of many, many of my own trials and errors in quilting.

When I use the word contrast, I am referring to opposite elements. You can use opposite densities, colors, and designs to create or enhance contrast in a quilt. It's as simple as picking opposites!

Fill in the background with swirls or try a variety of designs.

Straight lines coming from star

Maybe a pointy design in the background

Try wavy lines.

Hide different designs in the background quilting.

Background design can be smaller than the radiating designs.

Experiment with different designs.

Swirly designs radiating from other star

Quilting to Create Contrast

In a quilt made out of fabrics that are similar in value, the piecing may tend to blend together. Quilting can help define the pattern of the quilt by adding contrast between the different sections.

To provide contrast on the quilt pictured at right, I quilted the darker part using a dense, swirly design. In the lighter areas, I quilted an opposite design of straight lines that follow the piecing pattern.

Quilting can help define the quilt pattern.

Quilting to Emphasize Existing Contrast

Quilting can help define a quilt pattern by adding contrast, but it can also take away from a quilt that already has good contrast. On a quilt with distinct contrasting colors, an allover quilting design can be distracting.

Most often the best choice is to use different thread colors to match the different parts of the quilt top. At the very least, try to find a thread color that blends with much of the entire quilt.

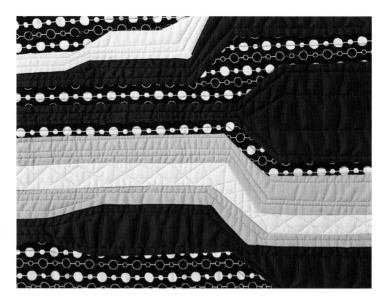

Take, for instance, the contrast quilt pictured at right. This quilt already has a lot of contrast, making the quilt pattern easy to see. Instead of quilting an allover pattern, I opted to quilt different designs in each section.

Contrast within Quilting Designs

Lack of contrast in the piecing isn't the only thing you need to look for. If you are quilting motifs, you want to have enough contrast in the quilting that the motifs will show up.

To demonstrate what I mean, I quilted the same design twice using different amounts of contrast. The first photo shows a quilting design that doesn't have enough contrast. The filler quilting around the central motif is almost the same size as the motif itself, making the main design difficult to see.

The quilting motif blends in because of a lack of contrast with the filler stitching.

In the next photo, the motif is much easier to see because of better contrast between the quilting designs. Not only did I echo-stitch around the design to give some space between the motif and the filler, but I also made the filler stitching smaller than that of the motif. This helps the eye pick out the design much more easily.

Also, I quilted the main design in a slightly darker color in the second example. The contrast in color helps the motif stand out.

This may seem like a lot to consider when you are quilting, but it's definitely worth it! If you are going to take the time to quilt a design, you want to make sure that your quilting stands out.

Smaller designs surrounding the central motif make it more prominent.

How to Create Contrast

When trying to create the most contrast between quilting designs, consider the following:

- **Color:** Use slightly differing colors of thread to provide contrast.

- **Density:** Make one design bigger than the other to automatically help the two designs stand apart.

- **Design:** Juxtapose different designs to create contrast—straight lines next to curvier designs, for example.

Consider using different quilting designs in different sections.

Fire and Ice

FINISHED SIZE: 47½˝ × 64½˝ • Finished block size: 20˝ × 20˝

Pieced and machine quilted by Angela Walters

Just being aware of the difference that contrast can make in a quilt will set you on the right path to selecting the quilting designs for *Fire and Ice.* Bold abstract stars contrast with each other and with the more subdued quilt background, offering plenty of cues for contrasting quilting styles.

MATERIALS

Tan (background): 3¼ yards

Scraps of various blue shades (blue star)

Scraps of various red and orange shades (orange star)

Beige (binding): ½ yard

Backing: 3¼ yards

Batting: 55″ × 72″

CUTTING

Tan

Cut 8 squares 11″ × 11″.

Cut 2 rectangles 20½″ × 23½″.

Cut 2 rectangles 4½″ × 47½″.

Cut 2 rectangles 4½″ × 20½″.

Cut 1 rectangle 16½″ × 47½″.

Blue and red/orange

Cut 4 strips of each color in sizes ranging in width from 1″ to 3″ and in length from 5″ to 16″.

Beige

Cut 7 strips 2¼″ × width of fabric for binding.

Making the Star Blocks

1. On an 11″ × 11″ tan square, use a pencil or erasable fabric marker to draw a line from a corner diagonally to the opposite corner. Place an orange strip facedown so that the raw edge overlaps the line by approximately ¼″.

2. Using a ¼″ seam allowance, sew the orange strip in place along the drawn line. Press the strip open.

Stitch along the diagonal line.

3. Place another fabric strip facedown on the first strip. Angle it so its top edge is lower on the first side than on the other, making sure it remains on top of the orange strip. Sew together along the edge of the top strip, using a ¼″ seam allowance. Press open.

4. Repeat the process until half the block is covered with angled strips. Trim the block to 10½″ × 10½″.

5. Repeat Steps 1–4 to make 3 more red/orange blocks.

6. Sew the 4 blocks together with the tan halves facing out, rotating them so the center forms a star.

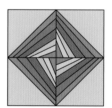

7. Repeat the process to make 4 blocks using the blue fabrics, and sew them together in the same way.

Assembling the Quilt

1. Sew a 4½˝ × 20½˝ rectangle of tan fabric to the left side of each star block.

2. Sew a 20½˝ × 23½˝ rectangle of background fabric to the right side of each star block.

3. Sew a 4½˝ × 47½˝ strip of background fabric to the top of each star unit.

4. Referring to the quilt top assembly diagram, turn the blue star section upside down and then join the 2 star sections with a 16½˝ × 47½˝ strip of tan background fabric.

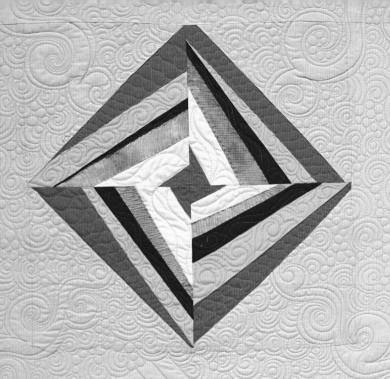

The Quilting

Layer the top, batting, and backing.

This quilt is all about contrast, and the quilting is no different. When selecting the quilting designs, I knew I wanted to have contrast in the types of designs as well as in the color of thread. The result is a quilt that has contrast on every level!

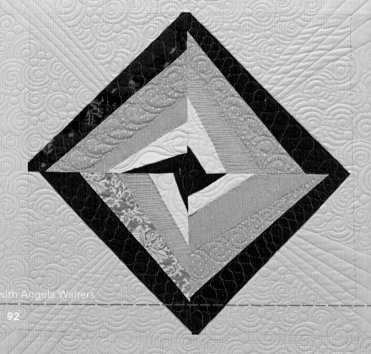

Quilting the Stars

Within each star, I quilted the same designs with thread that matches the fabric. But the quilting that extends out from the star is a whole different story.

The molten-hot orange star has a swirl design radiating out from each side. The design starts small but grows larger as it gets farther from the block. I used a light orange thread just a few shades darker than the tan background. I wanted just a little contrast; too dark a thread would have detracted from the block.

The ice-cold blue star has piercing straight lines radiating out from the block. As with the orange block, the lines are a little closer together at the beginning and then spread apart as they travel outward. This time I used a pale blue thread to add just a touch of contrast.

I don't often mark my quilt tops, but this quilt is one that you'll want to consider marking. Using a ruler, draw straight lines radiating out from the stars. These lines will act as guides to keep your quilting design on track.

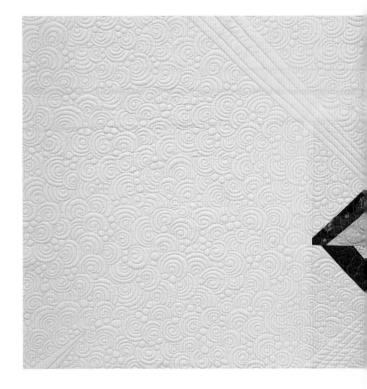

Quilting the Background

Because I wanted to make sure that the main quilting would show up, I quilted the background with a smaller swirl design. I also used a thread that matches the background fabric. Because I can never leave well enough alone, I threw some fun details in the background quilting: I quilted three shooting stars (to represent my children) and stars in two of the corners. It is a space-themed quilt, after all!

Finishing

When you are finished with the quilting, remove the guide marks you made on the quilt top, following the directions from the marking tool's manufacturer. Use your favorite method to attach the binding.

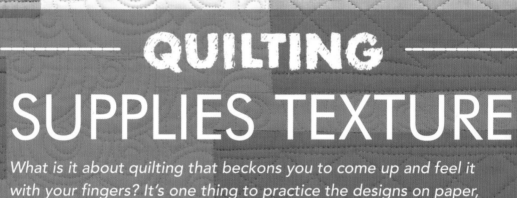

QUILTING
SUPPLIES TEXTURE

What is it about quilting that beckons you to come up and feel it with your fingers? It's one thing to practice the designs on paper, but it's a whole different thing to see them come to life on the quilt. The texture that quilting contributes is what gives the quilt such a finished look.

Using the quilting to create texture is a way of adding another layer of art to a quilt. All you have to do is to be mindful of the designs that you are using.

Tight back-and-forth lines add a lot of texture.

Maybe try a paisley quilting design.

Try several of your favorite designs in the blocks.

Keep spacing consistent.

Pick a consistent background design and use matching thread to add texture.

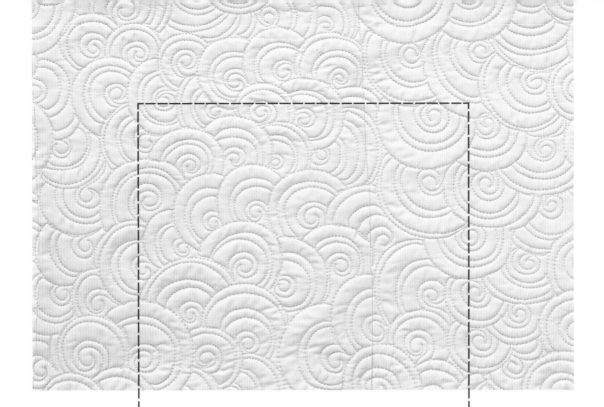

What Is Texture?

Texture, another element of art, can be used to describe either the way a quilt actually feels when you touch it or how it visually "feels" when you look at it. I love the idea of a quilt's visual feel—quilting that adds so much texture you can almost feel it just by looking at the quilt.

Great texture happens when you don't notice the quilting. Instead, you see the slight shadow and depth that the stitches give to the quilt top.

Tips for Great Texture

Quilting, by its nature, adds texture to a quilt; the following tips will help you make the most of that texture.

- **Concentrate on solid and near-solid fabrics.** When a quilt includes large areas of solid fabric, use a quilting design that adds texture. Since quilting doesn't show up as well on patterned fabrics, seek out the solid parts of the quilt so that your quilting will produce a lot of texture.

- **Use matching thread.** If the thread contrasts with the quilt top too much, a person will see the quilting rather than the texture. Consider using a thinner thread, too. The more a thread blends in, the better. Remember, great texture happens when the quilting "disappears" and the *shadow* of the quilting shows.

- **Use a consistent design.** If a design has a lot of variation in spacing, the design becomes the focus. Use dense quilting designs to play up texture—the more quilting, the more texture. If a design has a lot of open space, that open space will become the focus.

- **Think of designs in terms of a texture.** When choosing designs, think about the kind of texture you want to add to the quilt. Do you want linear texture, swirly texture, pointy texture? Considering this question will help you decide on the perfect quilting design.

- **Vary the design to add texture.** Texture isn't the same as an allover design. Simply quilting one design, whether it's an allover pattern or a custom design, won't necessarily add the texture you want. Use designs that change the texture, even just a little bit, in parts of your quilt to create more interest.

What Does Texture Look Like?

Defining texture is kind of like defining love. It's hard to explain, but you know it when you see it! So to help illustrate it, I heavily quilted the left side of a quilt block, creating amazing texture, and I less intricately quilted the other half, creating just so-so texture. Of course, how you decide to quilt is a matter of taste and the statement you want to make, but the goal is to have great texture.

On the left side of the block, I used matching thread and designs that are dense and consistent. The designs in each section are even and not distracting.

On the right side of the block, however, I used thread that didn't match as well and quilted designs that weren't as dense. I think the right side of the block looks great—there's definitely nothing wrong with it—but it doesn't have the textural quality that the other side has.

Basket Case

FINISHED SIZE: 65½˝ × 81¾˝

*Pieced by Mary Workman and Jessica Harrison,
and machine quilted by Angela Walters*

When I set out to design a project that would showcase texture, all I could think about was a quilt that incorporated a weave element. After many tries, I finally came up with *Basket Case*, not your typical woven-looking quilt. With plenty of background area to showcase your favorite quilting design, this quilt will have people wanting to run their hands over it!

MATERIALS

Cream solid (for background):
5 yards with at least 42″ usable width

Blue solids (for blocks and binding):
2 shades totaling 2⅛ yards

Batting: 74″ × 90″

Backing: 5⅛ yards

CUTTING

Cream solid

Cut 14 strips
1¼″ × width of fabric.

Cut 13 strips 3¾″ × width of fabric; subcut as follows:

For 8″ columns—

30 segments 1¾″ × 3¾″

32 segments 2½″ × 3¾″

26 segments 3¼″ × 3¾″

For 11″ columns—

20 segments 1¾″ × 3¾″

20 segments 3″ × 3¾″

20 segments 3¾″ × 3¾″

16 segments 4½″ × 3¾″

Cut 2 strips 8″ × length of fabric (after you have cut the above strips); subcut into

8″ × 5½″ (Column 1a)

8″ × 34½″ (Column 1b)

8″ × 59″ (Column 2)

8″ × 15¾″ (Column 5a)

8″ × 11¼″ (Column 5b)

8″ × 5¼″ (Column 8a)

8″ × 31½″ (Column 8b)

Cut 1 strip 4″ × 81¾″
(Column 6; cut lengthwise).

Cut 2 strips 11″ × length of fabric; subcut into

11″ × 13¾″ (Row 3a)

11″ × 39¼″ (Row 3b)

11″ × 34¾″ (Row 7a)

11″ × 18¼″ (Row 7b)

Blue solids

Cut 14 strips 3″ × width of fabric.

Cut 8 strips 2¼″ × width of fabric for binding.

tip *Cutting multiple strips at once will make the process go much more quickly.*

Making the Quilt

1. Sew a cream strip 1¼″ × width of fabric to a blue strip. Press carefully. Repeat with the remaining 1¼″ cream strips and the remaining blue strips to make a total of 14 strip units.

2. Subcut the strips as follows:

For the 8″ column—

7 strips 8″ long

15 strips 5½″ long

16 strips 4″ long

13 strips 2½″ long

For the 11″ column—

5 strips 11″ long

10 strips 8½″ long

10 strips 6″ long

10 strips 4½″ long

8 strips 3″ long

3. Sew each size of blue-and-cream strip to the appropriate cream side pieces as shown in the diagrams below.

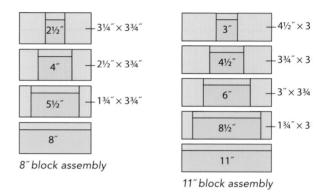

8″ block assembly

11″ block assembly

4. Piece the columns as shown in the quilt top assembly diagram below. Then sew the columns together in the indicated order to finish the quilt top.

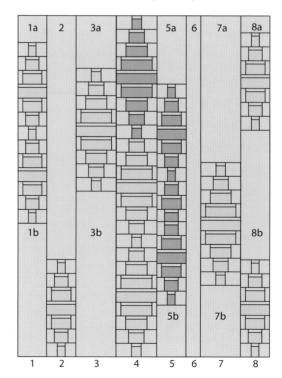

The Quilting

Layer the top, batting, and backing.

The choice of solid fabric for this quilt was not an accident! I wanted to be sure that the texture that quilting adds could be seen.

Quilting the Background

Because dense quilting patterns seem to provide the best texture, I used a variation of the concentric circle design for the background area. The only difference is the spacing of the rings. I alternated between ⅛″ and ¼″ between the rings. If you had been in the room while I was quilting, you would have heard me reminding myself out loud, "Close, far, close, far …"

To add the most texture, I used matching thread and tried to keep the designs consistent.

Quilting the Blocks

Within the blue sections, I used a thin thread that blends in. I quilted two different designs, each of them adding a different texture. I think the design that looks like building blocks adds the most texture.

Finishing

When you have completed the quilting, use your favorite method to attach the binding.

If you want to add the ultimate amount of texture, throw the quilt into the washer and then bask in all the resulting crinkly goodness!

QUILTING

ADDS COLOR

I spend so much time matching thread colors to quilt tops that sometimes I overlook the fact that quilting can actually add color to a quilt.
But every once in a while I come across a quilt that is just begging for
brightly colored thread. In this chapter I'll show you different ways
to add color to such quilts. So pull out your craziest threads and get
ready for some colorific quilting!

Before we start, I want to clarify. I'm not talking here about thread
painting. Thread painting is when a quilter uses only thread to make
a design. Quilts that include thread painting are obviously stunning.
But the purpose of this chapter is to show how you can use thread
colors to enhance the quilt pattern.

Try a variety of designs and thread colors—the more the better!

Use matching thread so as not to distract from piecing.

Large amount of negative space means you can experiment with fun designs.

Maybe alternating designs?

Super-sized swirls are an option.

Try designs in different sizes.

Try extending the quilting beyond the wedge.

Combine designs.

Thread Types

I love thread—that's no secret. My motto is, "If quilting is my therapy, then threads are my meds!" The many different kinds of threads that are available can be mind-blowing. The kind of thread that you want to use depends on how much color you wish to add and how distinctly you want it to show up.

Cotton

Cotton thread usually has a thickness that will show up on a quilt. This is great when you really want the color to stand out and be noticed.

Specialty Threads

The bling of quilting, specialty threads can be a lot of fun to use. Glitter threads, variegated threads, and glow-in-the-dark threads are just a few examples of specialty threads. Though fun and different, these threads can be finicky to deal with. I suggest trying a small spool before you invest in a large cone.

Polyester

Poly thread is usually much thinner than cotton, which makes it great for adding hints of color. Polyester threads can be shiny or matte, depending on the brand.

Making a Thread Book

When you are an avid thread collector, like me, it can be hard to remember exactly how the thread will look when actually quilted on a quilt top. I have several thread cards handy, but sometimes they aren't much help.

What I have done is to make a thread book—a quilted sampler of different threads and colors. The great thing about having an actual quilted sample is that I can see exactly what the thread will look like when it's quilted. No more guesswork or painful unquilting!

Making a thread book is super easy and well worth it. On a white or light-colored fabric, draw squares with a water-soluble marker. Quilt within each box using a different thread. Write the thread information on the back of each square to help you remember which thread you used on each square.

Carefully cut apart the quilted squares on the lines you drew. Stack the squares on top of each other and sew along one of the edges to make a book. Keep it next to your sewing machine or quilting machine to use as a reference for selecting thread.

> **tip** *Making a thread book is a great way to practice different free-motion quilting designs!*

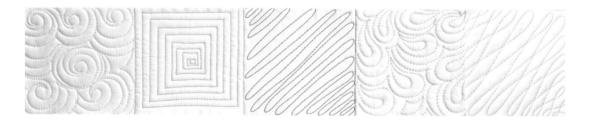

Putting Color to Work

You can use colorful quilting to do any or all of the following:

- **Add interest to a quilt.** As I've said about a million times, matching thread is my favorite! But every so often I see a quilt that could use a pop of color. You can use color to draw attention to an area or to balance a quilt that has a lot of color in one section but not in the rest of the quilt.

- **Change the quilt's appearance.** Sometimes I piece an entire quilt, only to find that one fabric doesn't quite work in the quilt. Thread color can help camouflage those "problem" spots.

- **Create a different look.** When using quilting to add color to a quilt, you don't have to use a *lot* of color. Just a little bit, used the right way, can give a whole different look to a quilt. In the case of the checkerboard quilt at right, a little strategically placed color added a great deal.

With various orange shades on one side and green shades on the other, I thought the center of the quilt could use a little color as well. So I whipped out my brightest orange and green threads and added a checkerboard pattern. Even though the quilting changes the look of the quilt, it still doesn't overwhelm the bold colors on the sides.

Of course, this is just one example of how to add color to a quilt pattern with quilting. The possibilities are limitless!

Some Last Thoughts

Try More Than One Color
If you really want to add color and make the quilting pop, consider using more than one color of thread. This is especially effective with contrasting colors.

Use more than one thread color for an even more colorful quilt.

The sample pictured above is a great example of using more than a single thread color on a quilt. I quilted a swirly design with two different thread colors. The

bright threads stand out against the black background, really helping to showcase the quilting. But to keep the color from being overwhelming, I quilted around the pieced designs with thread that matched the fabric.

But Don't Go Crazy
Using a contrasting thread to add color doesn't mean that you have to use it everywhere. A contrasting thread color looks best when used thoughtfully and sparingly.

Spin Doctor

FINISHED SIZE: 60½″ × 72½″

Pieced and machine quilted by Angela Walters

Now that you've learned all sorts of ways to add color with quilting, it's time to put that knowledge into practice. A fun and quick quilt to make, *Spin Doctor* allows you to experiment with different threads and colors to make the center seem to spin right off the quilt!

MATERIALS

Gray solid (for background and binding): 3¾ yards

Assorted grays and blacks (for wheel wedges): 2½ yards total

Black solid (for center): 1 fat quarter

Backing: 3¾ yards

Batting: 68″ × 80″

Fusible interfacing

Large circular item (such as a mixing bowl) to use as a pattern

Pen or marker

CUTTING

Gray

Cut 2 rectangles 36½″ × 60½″.

tip *Set aside the left-over gray fabric to use toward creating 2¼″-wide binding strips—you will need about 8 yards of binding.*

Assorted grays and blacks

Cut about 45 rectangles 3½″ × 20″ from a range of gray and black fabrics.

Black fabric

Trace around the circular object onto the black fabric. Cut out the circle, adding ½″ all around. The cut-out circle should be bigger around than the object.

Making the Wedges

1. Fold a rectangle of black or gray fabric in half lengthwise so that the edges line up.

2. Line up a ruler from the top corner (opposite the fold) to the bottom on the opposite side, approximately ½˝ from the fold. Using a rotary cutter, cut along the ruler.

3. Unfold the wedge and use scissors to cut a gentle outward curve at the top (wider) end.

4. Follow the same steps to make wedges out of all the gray and black rectangles.

tip *You might have to cut more wedges, but 45 is a good starting point.*

Assembling the Quilt

1. Sew the 2 gray 36½˝ × 60½˝ rectangles together lengthwise to make the 60½˝ × 72½˝ background.

2. Using the circular item as a pattern, lightly trace a circle onto the background fabric with a pen, making sure the center of the quilt is exactly in the middle of the circle. This is your guide for placing the wedges.

3. Begin positioning the wedges so that the bottom of each wedge is touching the circle drawn on the quilt. Start by placing wedges at the 4 compass points as guides for the rest of the pieces.

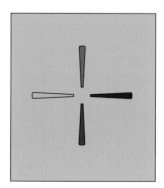

4. Position the rest of the wedges around the circle, slightly overlapping the edges. To make sure all the wedges point out at an accurate right angle, the center of the bottom of the wedge should point toward the center of the quilt.

To put your own spin on this quilt, overlap the wedges to make some appear narrower, leave spaces between a few wedges, and trim the tops of some to make them shorter. The more random the wedges appear, the better.

NOTE: Overlapping the wedges slightly will ensure that the background fabric won't show through when you start quilting.

5. Once you are happy with the way the wedges are laid out, use fusible interfacing to attach them to the quilt top, following the manufacturer's directions.

6. Fuse the black circle onto the center of the quilt so it covers up the bottom ends of the wedges.

7. Secure the wedges by sewing along the edges of each shape—or, if you will be quilting right away, secure them during the quilting process.

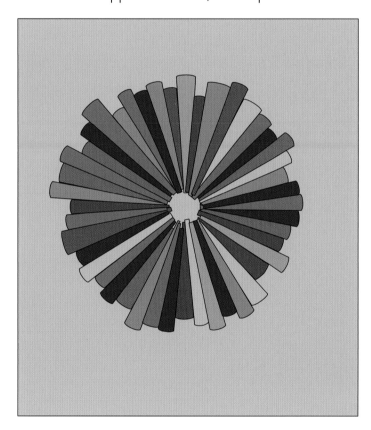

The Quilting

Layer the top, batting, and backing.

Quilting the *Spin Doctor quilt* offered me a great opportunity to use all the colorful threads that I seem to collect but never use!

A word of warning before you begin: Because pieces of this quilt are fused in place, some areas will have several layers of fabric and fusible interfacing. This can make the quilting a little tricky. In those areas, quilting more slowly or using a larger needle will help make the process a little easier.

Quilting the Wedges

Because this quilt is made of gray and black fabrics, I used different-colored threads to add my own "spin." Before I started, I chose a few different designs to use in the wedges and a few different thread colors.

tip *Because the stitching will be very noticeable on this quilt, it's a good idea to pick quilting designs with which you feel quite comfortable.*

For the designs, I stuck to some of my favorites—wishbones, arcs, swirls, and wavy lines. I specifically chose designs that could easily fit the shape of the wedges. All of these designs use the edges of the pieces as a guide.

For the black circle in the center of the quilt, I quilted a large swirl in matching thread. I wanted something simple that wouldn't detract from the rest of the quilt.

Quilting the Background

Because the center is the dominant portion of the quilt, I didn't want the quilting in the background to distract from it. Actually, I wanted the quilting in the background to draw the viewer's eye *to* the center. To accomplish that, I quilted gentle wavy lines radiating from the center. And just because I can never leave well enough alone, I added circles between a few of the lines. The result is a design that is interesting but doesn't take away from the overall look of the quilt.

Finishing

When you have completed the quilting, use your favorite method to attach the binding.

QUILTING
GIVES A SENSE OF SCALE

When you want your quilting to be interesting but not overwhelming, consider using it to add scale to your quilt. I'm not talking about scales as in music. I'm talking about scale as a succession of steps or degrees. The same allover quilting design in different sizes, small to large, does the trick.

This technique is easy yet striking, and it will help you take your quilting to a new level. It adds interest to a quilt—especially those large areas of negative space that can be overwhelming—and moves the eye along, drawing attention to the most important parts of the quilt.

Quilting design smaller to bigger

Quilt each wedge with a different design.

Or quilt each section with one design.

Blending thread for background

Pick just two designs and alternate.

Mark lines to separate different sizes of quilting.

Experiment with several different designs to get some practice.

Use the same thread in sections or try a fun, colored thread.

Maybe swirls? Most designs work well.

Adding Scale to a Quilt

Perhaps the best thing about using quilting to add scale is that takes just a little more effort than an ordinary allover design, yet it still contributes a great deal to the artistry of the quilt. Chances are you'll find even more variations than I have suggested here.

First, Mark the Quilt

Decide how much gradation you want. The more sizes you use, the more variation there will be from the smallest to the largest designs. Roughly divide the quilt into the same number of sections as design sizes. This will help you stay organized, because after you start quilting it is very easy to lose track of what you are doing. Use a blue water-soluble marking pen to label the different sections.

The quilting design can progress in several different ways, as illustrated by the photos below.

Smaller in the middle, larger toward the edges

Smaller on top, larger on the bottom

Smaller in one top corner, larger toward the opposite bottom corner

Smaller in the middle, larger toward the edges

Pick a Design

Almost any allover design works well for this technique. If you can quilt it in many different sizes, then it will work. Circles, swirls, and feathers are just a few examples of successful designs. You can even quilt straight lines that start out being spaced closely together and get farther apart as you proceed.

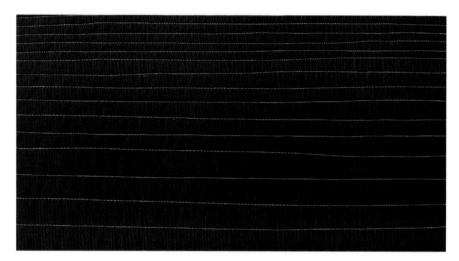

Draw a Guide

To keep yourself on track, draw the design in each size you'll be using, from smallest to largest, on paper. Keep the designs next to you while you quilt to help you keep the designs the right size.

Quilt It!

Now use the guide to begin quilting, moving to a new size in each successive section. While you are quilting, it may be hard to see the gradations in scale. But trust me, when you are finished and stand back to view your work, they will definitely be noticeable.

Mixing Two Designs

A different twist on this technique is to start with one quilting design and then gradually turn it into a different design.

Divide the quilt into three sections. The first section will be for the original design, the middle section will be a combination of the two designs, and the third section will be for the second design.

The center section that combines the two different designs allows them to transition gracefully without an abrupt change.

NOTE: *The different sections don't necessarily have to be the same size in a quilt that transitions from one design to another.*

Stacked

FINISHED SIZE: 50½″ × 60½″

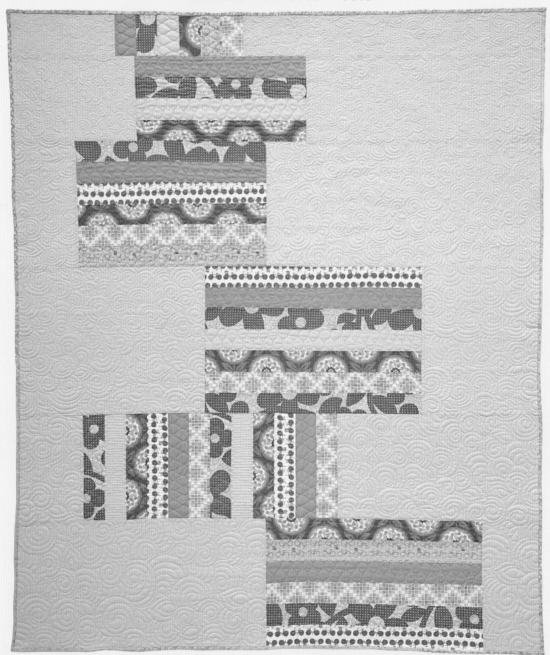

Pieced by Mary Workman and machine quilted by Angela Walters

This quilt pattern is designed to make the quilting process easy and speedy! It is jelly roll–friendly and a great way to showcase some of your favorite print fabrics.

MATERIALS

Pink solid (for background): 2 yards

Mixed prints (for striped blocks): 1¾ yards total, the more different fabrics the better

Binding: ½ yard

Backing: 3¼ yards

Batting: 57″ × 67″

CUTTING

Mixed prints

Cut 12 strips 2½″ × width of fabric.

Cut 7 strips 2½″ × 22½″.

Cut 4 strips 2½″ × 16½″.

Cut 7 strips 2¼″ × width of fabric for binding.

tip *Using sticky notes to label the various background sections will save you a lot of time when it comes to putting the quilt top together.*

Pink

Cut 1 strip 4½″ × width of fabric; subcut into

    1 rectangle 4½″ × 10½″ (Row 1a)

    1 rectangle 4½″ × 28½″ (Row 1b)

Cut 1 strip 10½″ × width of fabric; subcut into

    1 rectangle 10½″ × 14½″ (Row 4b)

    1 rectangle 10½″ × 6½″ (Row 5a)

    1 rectangle 10½″ × 20½″ (Row 5b)

Cut 2 strips 12½″ × width of fabric; subcut into

    2 rectangles 12½″ × 6½″ (Rows 3a and 6b)

    1 rectangle 12½″ × 24½″ (Row 6a)

    1 rectangle 12½″ × 8½″ (Row 2a)

    1 rectangle 12½″ × 26½″ (Row 3b)

Cut 1 rectangle 8½″ × 22½″ (Row 2b)

Cut 1 rectangle 14½″ × 18½″ (Row 4a)

Making the Quilt Top

1. Randomly select 6 print width-of-fabric strips and sew them together along their long sides to form a single large piece measuring 12½″ × width of fabric. Carefully press the seams.

2. Repeat with 6 more width-of-fabric strips to form a second pieced strip the same size.

3. Subcut the first pieced strip into pieces 4½″ wide (Block 1), 10½″ wide (Block 5a), and 20½″ wide (Block 6).

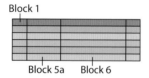

Block 1

Block 5a   Block 6

4. Subcut the second pieced strip into pieces 18½″ wide (Block 3) and 10½″ wide (Block 5b).

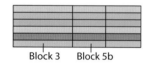

Block 3   Block 5b

5. Sew together the 4 print strips 2½″ × 16½″, long sides together, to make a block that measures 8½″ × 16½″ (Block 2).

6. Sew the 7 print strips 2½″ × 22½″ together along their long sides to make a block that measures 14½″ × 22½″ (Block 4).

7. Sew Blocks 5a and 5b together along their short edges to make Block 5.

8. Referring to the quilt top assembly diagram, sew each block to the corresponding background pieces to form rows. Stitch the rows together to complete the quilt top.

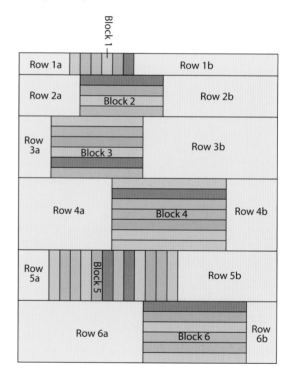

The Quilting

Layer the top, batting, and backing.

From the smallest block at the top to the biggest block on the bottom, this quilt is all about scale! The quilting is no exception. Use the quilt's design as inspiration for your quilting to emphasize scale.

Quilting the Background

Because the quilt is pieced in strips, you already have guidelines for the quilting. This means that you don't have to mark the quilt to make the design smaller at the top and bigger at the bottom.

NOTE: *For this quilt I made my designs smaller on the top and larger on the bottom to mimic the changing scale of the quilt blocks. But you could easily have the different design sizes go from left to right. Just make guidelines with a water-soluble pen to mark where you want to change sizes.*

For the background quilting, I combined two different designs: a swirl and a leaf. First I drew the designs in six different sizes on a piece of paper, from smallest to largest, to use as a guide. I kept the guide next to me as I quilted so that I could be sure my designs remained as consistent as possible.

I quilted the smallest design in the first row of the background, the second-smallest design on the second row, and so on, ending with the largest design on the last (bottom) row.

The background quilting consists of swirls and a leaf design.

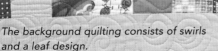

Stacked

Quilting the Blocks

Quilting in the Stacked *blocks mixes two designs.*

For quilting the strips within the blocks, I alternated between a wishbone design and a back-and-forth line. Though these were the designs I used, a number of other patterns would work equally well. Experiment with your own favorites.

Of course, you don't have to quilt the blocks differently from the background. If you prefer, you can treat the background quilting pattern as an allover design and use it in the blocks as well.

Finishing

After you have completed the quilting, use your favorite method to attach the binding.

About the Author

Angela Walters is a machine quilter and author who loves to teach others to use quilting to bring out the best in their quilt tops. Her work has been published in numerous magazines and books. She shares tips and finished quilts on her blog, quiltingismytherapy.com, and believes that "quilting is the funnest part!"

Also by Angela Walters

Also available as an ebook